THIS BOOK BELONGS
— to —
Paul
Massie

120 Years Of Changes

1880-2000

Dedicated to Our Children
Carolyn, Paul & Randy

Louise K. Nelson
Mazie K. Gerringer

Best Regards
Louise K. Nelson
Mazie K. Gerringer

Publisher: Louise K. Nelson
Cover Design: Louise K. Nelson-Debbie Carpenter
Interior Design: Louise K. Nelson- Debbie Carpenter
Copyrighted: 2000 Louise K. Nelson
Printed in The United States of America

ISBN 09671476-4-6

Library of Congress Number 2001-130549

The book may be purchased from dealers or by calling the author. Ordering information page 226

Other books available by the author:
    Country Folklore 1997
    The Aroma & Memories of Grandma's and Mama's Kitchen
1998
    Horse Drawn Equipment & Early Tools 1999
    Historic Waynesville & Haywood County 1999

Louise K. Nelson
1336 Asheville Rd.
Waynesville, NC 28786

828-456-3760

Contents

Introduction

To

120 Years of Changes

This being a book I have had in mind since I began writing has finally become a reality.

I used my family as an example. The main character is my Grandpa, Wiley Caldwell.

The book begins with the years 1880 when Wiley's parents were married. It tells of their struggle to survive.

Then it tells of Wiley's struggle of living, beginning at his birth 1886. It tells how very poor the family was and how they had to eventually farm the boys, Wiley and his brother Bill Caldwell out.

It tells of the years when they had no education. Also it tells how the area where they lived had wild animals and how some of the wild animals were used for meat.

Wiley went through these years of changes in farm equipment. It tells how the farms changed from oxen to horses, how it changed from handmade equipment to horse drawn and then to the modern days of machinery.

Then it tells how Wiley and Dollie Caldwell had to adapt to an easier way of life with electricity.

It goes through the country and town changes. After electricity there were too many changes to tell about. We have named a lot of them.

My sister, Mazie K. Gerringer co-authored this book with me. She tells how she remembers the last 56 years.

Louise K. Nelson   Mazie K. Gerringer

Early
Country Years

Walker log house, Fines Creek c-1875

Ways of Living Before The Years 1880

Wiley's parents were born in the years 1858-1860. His grandparents (The Caldwell's) were from North Carolina. His grandparents (The Owens) were from Tennessee.

They lived in hewn log cabins with mud chinking between the logs. The chimneys were made of rocks and mud.

Wood was plentiful and it was used in many ways. To mention a few: the oxen yokes, rail fences, toilets, buildings to house the animals, and a barn. Sleds were made from wood and later wagons. Some of the early tools were made from wood. They soon learned to make plows, wood harrows, and equipment for the oxen to pull.

Rock was very useful in the fact that it also helped in making tools and in use of building fences and buildings.

His grandparents came to Haywood County to live in the early 1800s. In the country where they lived, there were many wild animals. A lot of them were used for meat for their meals. Many of the animals were dangerous and little by little, they killed them off to protect their livestock and their chickens. Some of the dangerous animals were: panthers, coyotes, bears, wildcats (bob cats), and wolves. Some of the animals that they ate were: wild turkeys, rabbits, squirrels and groundhogs. Some hides were used to make leather for shoes and clothes.

8

There were many poisonous snakes like copperheads and rattlesnakes.

Fish were plentiful and they were a good source of meat.

The families had a few guns and handmade knives.

They had used their handmade traps in capturing some of the animals.

Wiley tells how his grandparents never let the fire go out because there were no matches. When a person came for a short visit, they were asked,

"Did you come to borrow some coals?" This old saying was still around when I was growing up. They used flint stones rubbed together to start a fire. Can you imagine not having any matches?

Their light came from burning pine knots that were full of rosin.

There were many baths taken in the branches. Some folks were lucky enough to have wooden tubs.

Many folks traveled and spent the nights wherever they could. Bed bugs called "chinches" were around. They were carried from person to person. They were very hard to get rid of. The means of getting rid of them was to scour the house with homemade lye soap. The old saying from those days was, "Don't let the bed bugs bite".

Preservering fruits and vegetables were done by putting them in the sun to dry. Apples were smoked (or bleached) by burning sulphur. Vegetables were pickled. Then fruits and vegetables were buried in straw in the ground to save for winter use.

Everything had to be done right or there wasn't enough food to carry them through the winter.

Houses were cold because of the dirt floors and no insulation.

Donated photo

Handmade plows

Donated photo

Wooden fence and wooden harrow

The Rugged Years Beginning 1880

Wiley's parents, Greenberry and Sarah Owens Caldwell began their married life around 1880.

They started in a remote primitive farm area,

Hurricane Creek at Fines Creek in Haywood County, N.C.

They had moved into an old log cabin with hewn logs that had been put together with mud. The house was very old and the floor was dirt. It was in a shabby condition. The cabin was just one room with one door and two windows.

A few pieces of furniture had been given to them: 2 bedsteads (beds), 2 cheers (chairs), a bench, eatin' table, wash table, cupboard and a flour and meal bin.

Their means of cooking was from the fireplace. In the coals was a pan called an oven for baking bread. Coals covered the lid and were put around the pan to heat for baking the bread.

Sitting on the wash table was a wash pan, and a bucket of water with a gourd dipper.

There were a few necessary buildings as a toilet and a springhouse with a trough to hold milk and butter. There was an old log barn.

Soon they would need to find a wash pot and a wooden tub for washing clothes. They could use the wooden tub for getting a bath.

They had been taught to make lye soap from their old lard and lye that was made from ashes and water. Water seeped through the ashes until it turned into lye.

The men folks had learned to farm with oxen. They grew potatoes, corn and vegetables. The women folks had learned to preserve foods.

This was a rough way to start a marriage. It was the way their parents had started. It had to be hard keeping the body clean because there was no privacy in getting a bath. A lot of bathing was done in the creek or the branch. Lye soap had to be harsh. I was told that rubbing sand on the body would remove dirt also.

This old house is still standing, near the Iron Tree Golf Course. My grandparents, (Kinslands) lived here.

Log barn and log building from the past.

To tighten up the cords on the bed. With the cords tight the bed was firmer and sleeping was better. Thus the saying "Sleep tight".

Donated Photo
(Courtesy of the King Family) Old log house graduated from shingle roof to a tin roof. Kitchen was added later.

Wiley's Grandma Owens
Year approx 1884

Wiley was born to Sarah and Greenberry Caldwell in 1886. More children had been born to them and it was time for another child to be born.

Sarah's mother, (Grandma Owens) lived in Tennessee. She came to their home at Hurricane Creek to help in delivering the baby.

This part of the story will be told as Wiley, (My Grandfather), told me. This is the typical speech of Wiley's grandparents, his parents, and Wiley's generation. The speech started changing with my generation. We had schools and were taught a better speech. However, this language was instilled in our lives and we still use a lot of it.

Wiley's Story: "Grandma started rail early in the morning. She stopped at friends and staid th night. It wus a fur piece frum Tennessee. She come through the woods and fields. She carried a little dab uf food to eat. It was purtnear dark when she got to our house. She was tard, but she had to tell us all th news frum th family.

The baby wus born but Grandma staid longer because she wanted to put up Mother's pickle beans afore she left.

She headed back to Tennessee rail early in the morning. She wus going to stay all night with Henry Justice and his wife.

Efter a week or so the folks frum Tennessee come to see why she had not come home. They stopped at Henry Justice's house and Grandma Owens had not been there. They decided when they got to our house that they would start when th roosters begin crowing in th morning and they would look fur her. I wus a young boy but I know they thought sumthin had happened to her.

The men folks put food in a poke and said they might haf to look all day. It wusn't long until they saw Grandma's kerchief hanging in a bush! Then they found her handkerchief and it did not have her little dab uf money in it! There wus Grandma's body laying under the bush !

They took Grandma's body back to Tennessee on a sled. They buried her there."

These are some of the words that I remember them using:

Fruit- (Apples)

Maters- (Tomatoes)

Taters- (Potatoes)

Fetch- (Bring)

Roast Neers- (Boiled ears of corn)

Nubbin's - (Small ears of corn)

Runt- (The smallest pig)

Long Johns- (Men's long underwear)

Brung - (Brought)

Wus-(Was)

Staid- (Stayed)
Rail- (Real)
Sumthin- (Something)
Eatin'- (Eating)
Efter- (After)
Directly- (After a while)
Fixing to- (Starting to
Dark as pitch
Crack of dawn
Big day light

Struggling Years

Sarah and Greenberry Caldwell had a hard time keeping food on the table. Her life was very busy taking care of the children. She was sad because she knew there wasn't hardly enough food for the family.

The older girls helped in any way they could. They had all learned to milk the cows and churn to make butter and buttermilk. They helped take care of the younger children. What few clothes they had, they kept them washed.

The boys, Wiley and Bill had learned to plow. They now had a horse instead of the oxen. They kept the wood sawed and chopped for firewood.

19

The house had become very crowded. There was no school near by. The children had no education.

Sarah and Greenberry knew they must do something to help the children. They could not go on for long.

Other families had to farm their boys out. Being farmed out meant that they went to live with farmers for room, board and food.

The time had come when they must let the boys go with other people. Bill was farmed out to a family in Leicester, North Carolina. Wiley was farmed out to the Woody's at Cataloochee, North Carolina.

They knew there was nothing else they could do. At least the boys would have clothes and food.

With large families, what else could be done for their survival?

This era of life was very simple. Things seemed to be at a standstill for the poor people.

The Civil War

Ending in Haywood County May 9, 1865
Information by: Jim Howell

The years before Wiley was born and while Greenberry and Sarah were struggling to get on their feet, the Civil War had been a big loss to the Haywood County and to The Town Of Waynesville, North Carolina.

The Civil War had become history. Some of the men and boys that were away in the war came home wounded. The trains brought them to Morristown and Knoxville, Tennessee, or Morganton, North Carolina. They had to walk, lead the wounded, and carry some from the stations back to Haywood County.

George Kirk and the Raiders had burned homes, stole, and destroyed food. With the men and boys away, the women and the children had not been able to make crops for food. What they did have, they had to hide it from the Raiders.

Col. Bartlett set up camp at the White Sulphur Springs in Waynesville, N.C.

General Martin had got word to Col. Love and Col. Thomas to get organized.

General Martin had moved his troops from Asheville, N.C. The troops amounted to around 500. Some were sent to Balsam Gap and some to Soco Gap in the County.

Col. Love and his group (The Jim Conley Sharpshooters) were at Balsam Gap.

General Martin had Col. Thomas move his Indian Battalion from Qualla, in Cherokee,N.C. into Dellwood, N.C. after discovering Col. Bartlett's advance in Waynesville. They hoped to trap the enemies in town.

At this time Col. Love moved his group near White Sulphur Springs.

The sign tells the story.

The troops circled together and Col. Bartlett was alarmed by the Confederates.

On the night of May 6,1865 the troops were ordered to build fires on the slopes of the mountains so it would appear that lots of Confederates had joined them. Then the Indians began their war whoops and dances. After all these dances, whoops and fires, Col. Bartlett sent out a flag of truce.

Col. Bartlett and George Kirk and the Raiders were asked to leave town.

This was May 9, 1865.

While all of this was going on Gen. Martin had word that the war was over. It had been over a month, but there was no way to receive the message other than someone coming through on horseback.

The war had caused a lot of damage. The town and county had a struggle to get things started back.

2nd Lt. George Holland Nelson, (My husband, Floyd Nelson's, grandfather) had been among the service men that were in other parts with the Civil War. He was with the 2nd Regiment Co. of Haywood County, N.C.

2nd Lt. George Holland Nelson was captured when he returned to his home at Cataloochee, N.C. There was a companion with him. They were put under the school building with dirt to enclose them. Little by little they dug the dirt away to free themselves.

By the turn of the century, the town of Waynesville and the county had started gaining back their loss from the war and the struggling years.

Cataloochee and the surrounding sections of the town and the county had built larger houses. They were gaining by selling produce and livestock. The poor were struggling but gaining somewhat.

There were many changes in the businesses and building of new homes.

Move To Cataloochee,N.C.

This was around the turn of the century when Wiley began his living as a farmed out child from the Greenberry Caldwell family.

Wiley was now 14 years old. He was a heavy, robust fellow and could manage a day's work without any trouble. He was very sad because he missed his family.

The larger farmers were thriving from the sale of pigs, livestock, sheep, chickens, and produce. They were building nice, larger homes. A lot of the smaller farmers and tenants still lived in old log homes that were falling apart.

The lands had been cleared because there were many crops. The wild animals had been killed somewhat and livestock was secure in the fenced pastures.

The farmers needed help to take care of the large farms. A cattle trail had been cut through the mountains from Cataloochee to Clyde, NC. Roads would soon be opened.

A group of men in wagons would go ahead of the drovers and they would find a spot to camp out and to cook their meals. This would be the spot where the livestock would rest and where they would be fed.

The drovers had to be alert to keep the cattle together. The sheep had to be led because they have no sense of directions.

They made this trip sometimes in winter months. The Pigeon River at Clyde would be slushy ice and sometimes it would be frozen. Their shoes and overalls would be wet. The shoes couldn't take much of the water to survive. By the time they arrived back at Cataloochee their shoes would be pretty well worn out.

The wagons would be empty of the feed for the livestock and of special things they had taken to the market like corn and vegetables. In return they brought back supplies, foods, and sometimes lumber for building.

The farmers and the cattle drovers had long days. Their days began before dawn and most of the time it would be dark before the livestock would be fed. The farmer could finally rest from a hard day's work. Wiley said he slept a lot of the time in the hayloft of the barn.

Wiley had been taught well by the Woodys. He knew how to farm, drive cattle and log wood. It was said that he could harness a team of mules and horses faster than a well-trained horseman. Not only had Wiley learned to manage the horses, he had been taught by his father to plow oxen as well. He had also been taught to build fences and make oxen yokes.

He said, "The oxen were slower than the horses. They were better at plowing, harrowing, pulling sleds, and wagons. The mules were very stubborn. They didn't want to always gee and haw when told to".

There were schools at Cataloochee, but Wiley was too old to begin and there was no time for schooling. He went to church at Cataloochee and he loved it. He would say, even in his older years, "It's time to go to the meeting house".

For a young fellow this was the art of living, learning and surviving.

The horses and mules had taken over the oxen. Seeing the train was a big change in Haywood County. This meant better means of transporting what the farmers grew to other parts of the world. Passenger trains were in all the cities adjacent to Waynesville, and of course Waynesville. The logging trains had begun in the mountains to move logs to the factories. Roads had become better. Framed houses were taking the place of the log homes. Schools were already better. This is some of the changes by the time Wiley finished his work at Cataloochee, N.C.

Palmer's Chapel-Cataloochee, N.C.

Old Cataloochee Church.

Caldwell's House and Barn, Cataloochee, N.C.

Cataloochee School

3 Jim Hannah log house, Little Cataloochee, 1864

JOHN NELSON LOG CABIN
Coggins Branch,
Cataloochee NC

Above: Jim Hannah log house, little Cataloochee
Below: John Nelson log cabin, Cataloochee

The Sawmill

Sam Lewis had a huge sawmill at Fines Creek, N.C. This is where Wiley found work.

The world was changing very much. The lumber from the sawmill would make good homes. The small log homes were going out. There were more larger and better-built homes. There were better barns and out buildings for storing the farmer's supplies and housing the animals.

Wiley worked as a logger. He had managed to use the horse to pull the logs. This was tricky, because the logs could roll over both the driver and the horse. The lumbermen would drag, skid, and get the logs out of the woods with a horse.

Some of the loggers lived back in the woods where they got the logs out. They cooked their meals on an open fire.

Wiley was one of the loggers that camped at the sawmill at the end of the day.

Wiley ate at the sawmill kitchen. He was a big eater. The meals were great!

While spending time at the kitchen he met a beautiful, brown-eyed girl, nineteen years old. The beautiful girl was Dollie Justice, who became his wife.

Dollie could neither read nor write, but she learned to cook by using a dab of this and a pinch of that.

Some of the foods were cathead biscuits, sawmill gravy, country ham, fruitcakes, potatoes and gravy, cornbread, buttermilk, butter, hog meat, chicken, and plenty of vegetables. A lot of the vegetables were fried, using hog grease.

Donated photo
For many years wooden barrels were used to store vegetables for the winter. Tubs were sometimes stored in the springhouse. Black wash pot was also used to cook large amounts of vegetables.

The sawmill was a big operation. The Lewis' hired farmers to make the crops, dairymen to take care of the cows and milking, loggers and cooks.

Everyone had their special jobs. Sunday was a time when the men folks would go fishing and then they had trout for meat.

When Wiley arrived at the sawmill he discovered that his father had been killed when someone was throwing pebbles and one hit him in the shoulder.

Some of his sisters had married. His brother, Bill was still living at Leicester where he had been farmed out. His mother was living with one of the daughters.

Wiley had an accident when a log rolled over his leg and injured it badly! He had surgery at the Waynesville Hospital. This kept him from doing the logging so he went to other farms for work.

He had been paid a small salary at the sawmill. This was enough to buy clothes, which he needed. His room and board was furnished.

Wiley's leg never completely healed. Some flesh was removed from above the knee and grafted in the wound. I'm sure he needed more medical service. These were the days when there was no means of money and no way to get to the doctor.

Over the years he developed diabetes and his wound opened up more. The last 20 years of his life it never healed.

There have been many changes in the medical field now. The hospitals are able to take care of any problem.

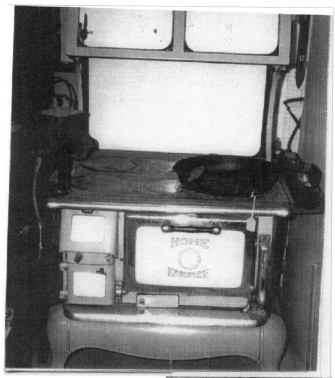

Wood cook stove.
Wiley's mother, Sara Owens
Caldwell with Pearl and Ann.
This is the only picture that
Wiley had. It was tucked
away in an old Bible.

Still Traveling Around

Wiley and Dollie could not seem to find the right place to live. They kept moving around. By now they had six children. One of the daughters remained living with the Lewis family.

A lot of people were going to South Carolina to work in a cotton mill. Wiley, Dollie, and five of the children sought work there.

Wiley didn't have the education to work in the mill. He worked in the fields of cotton. Wherever he worked, he did his best.

The older boys in the family were making some money, so was Wiley. This gave them a chance to buy a wood cook stove, two beds and necessary things that they needed.

The job in South Carolina was soon over, and all the farmers were moving back to the country to work as farmers.

This is the time that Wiley and Dollie started their life on Bill McCrary's farm at Big Branch in Haywood County. They were tenant farmers on the McCrary Farm.

They had their cook stove, beds, a sewing machine, and other pieces of furniture. They were gaining.

Wiley began working as a sharecropper. He earned a certain portion of the tobacco money, which was almost all the money they had. He was given half of the corn that was grown. This gave them plenty of meal for cornbread. He had a garden where they grew lots of vegetables. They raised hogs to have meat for the winter. Dollie set eggs under many hens so there would be lots of chickens and they would have plenty of eggs. Dollie preserved all the vegetables that she could and gathered all the nuts that grew wild. She saved, preserved, pickled, smoked, and dried vegetables and fruits. They had milk cows. There was plenty of milk to drink and to churn into butter and buttermilk. They had access to the wood that they needed to heat the house and use in the cook stove.

They, like their parents before them, buried vegetables and fruits covered in straw in the ground for winter use. They grew almost everything they had to eat.

Little by little, they were getting ahead in life and times were changing. It was great to not have to cook in the fireplace except when they wanted to. They had an old cook stove handed down to them before this, which was not very good; but now they had their own.

The buggies pulled by the horses had found their place in the barn loft. The tobacco crops were still planted by hand. The tobacco had to be wormed and suckered. The tobacco was hung in the shed or the barn loft to dry out.

When it came in case, which was cured and damp to handle, then it was worked up and waiting on the first tobacco market to open.

This was the era when there was an epidemic of diphtheria. Lots of people had died from it. Wiley and Dollie lost a daughter with this disease.

Wiley was getting satisfied with living where he was. Mr. McCrary knew he was a good worker. He was still a heavy, stout man. His nickname was "Biggin". Wiley was a man with a lot of strength. He could put a toe sack of corn or feed on his shoulder and carry it there.

The children helped Wiley and Dollie on the farm. Their daughter Flora, could do everything in the housework. She became the one that wanted to milk the cows.

Life went on. When they ran out of money they sold chickens and eggs, sometimes a country ham or maybe pigs.

Before the crack of dawn, Wiley and the boys would be out feeding the landlord's livestock. They would be getting ready to face a hard day of work on the farm. So much was still done by hand. Every plant was hoed. The now days tending of the crops are to spray with weed and bug killer. Not much hoeing is done now.

Before the men went to feed the livestock and the hogs, they built fires in the fireplace and cook stove.

Wiley insisted that someone look the signs up in the Almanac so he would know when the time was right for planting.

The hay was cut, hauled to the barn and stored in the hayloft or stacked in haystacks. The hay was pitched in the loft with a pitchfork. Corn was a must for the livestock feed and to be made into meal for cornbread. Straw from the wheat was placed in straw stacks and was used for filling the bed tick for sleeping on. The corn was still cut by hand. The fodder was pulled off the stalks, to feed to the livestock. The corn was shucked by hand. Then sometime later there were corn shuckers and silos. One of the changes was the corn shucks were no longer used to fill the bed ticks.

All the winter wood was sawed with a cross cut saw and chopped with an axe. The wood had to be brought from the woods with the help of the horses. The farmers carried a lot of tools to the woods when getting out wood for winter use.

All the shingles for the roofing were handmade. All the handles for hammers, sickle bars, ax and others were handmade.

The fence posts were split in the farmer's spare time for the fences. There was no barbwire fencing as yet.

Wood was used in many ways. Everything was made from a different wood. The bark from the white oak trees was used to make splits for bottoming chairs.

A special wood was used to make the shingle for the roof.

These are some of the tools that I remember Wiley and the men folks talking about: reap hooks, wheat cradles, splitting maul, froe, pole axe, double blade axe, fallin'axe, cross cut saw, hand saw, square, wedges, go-devils, crowbar, mallets, anvils, chisels, shovels, and peavy. They had handmade wagons and sleds. There were corn planters and tobacco ridgers and all kind of plows. I don't which of these tools went with the years of 1800s.

Donated photo
Rail fences were serviceable, made with split rails.
Wood was plentiful and was used in many ways.

Old cellar for storing foods.

Buggy from Francis Farm. Check book "*Horse Drawn Equipment and Early Tools*", by this author for many early photos.

Donated photo
Courtesy of Doyle Brown
The crosscut saw was used to cut firewood and stove wood.
The logs were hauled to the wood shed. It took two people
to pull the crosscut saw through the logs. Hand held mowing
sickle.

Hand bottomed chairs in the 1940s with split bark; by Shurman Justice.

Top: Gourd dipper
Bottom: Remains of an old unkept spring house. The trough
was used to store the milk and butter.

Donated photo

Early Sled and Shaver.

Gradual Changes

Changes were being made on the farm. They were proceeding by degrees. There were more and more changes in the variety of plows, still pulled by the horses and the mules. The wooden harrow had given way to the iron harrow.

The wheat mill and thrasher were out. Flour was being bought at the store. There was no more straw for straw ticks for sleeping on. Bush hogging and grubbing was still going on. In fact, there were so many jobs that still depended on the farmer's hand labor.

This was the year 1926 when the Home Extension of Haywood County came to the one–room school and taught the women folks to do canning of vegetables, fruits and meats in jars. The Ball Can Company offered a canning book that all the women ordered. They could follow the directions and it also told how long to cook in the open canner for each item. The canners held 7 or 12 cans.

This was a great change for the farmer's wives. Due to having no electricity for refrigeration the hog meat had to be eaten up before the warm weather began. It was great to can meat, lard, and cracklings. This would carry them through more months of saving food.

There were a few cars and trucks now coming into the Big Branch community. Drivers Licenses were still not required. This definitely was something special for the ones lucky enough to own a car.

Walking was still the thing to do in our family. We were still walking everywhere we went. Walking the four miles to and from church was not a problem since we were young.

The mules were still going around in circles pulling the old molasses mill to grind the cane until it became syrup to make molasses.

The women folks still made quilts. They were made out of necessity. If possible they secured sheep wool for the filling. The sheep were still being sheared and the landlord still sold the wool at the market.

The spinning wheel was resting in the corner of most homes, because materials could be bought to make quilt linings and clothes. However, we were still using feed and flour sacks to make dresses, underwear, towels, pillowcases, and sheets.

The handmade brogan shoes were over with. The men's shoes were made heavy but the children and the women's shoes were still sown together with thread. Our shoes or slippers were repaired at home on a last, by tacking the soles together with shoe tacks.

After killing the hogs, hams, fatback, and middling meat was stored in the smoke house.

There were still many animals on the farm. They all had their use for being there. Hogs were still the main source of meat. Chickens were the main source of summer meat. They stayed on foot until time to eat them.

The chickens were often sold to help with the expenses when the tobacco money ran out. The duck's feathers were used for making featherbeds and pillows.

The dogs herded the sheep and the cattle. The sheep were still used for wool. The horses and mules were still pulling the farm equipment. The guineas were for eggs. The turkeys were for meat.

There were many buildings around the farm to house all these animals. There were still many buildings around the farm for the farmers use and for the home use as: springhouse, smokehouse, cellar, toilet, corncrib, molasses shed, woodhouse, chicken houses, duck coops, barns, and cattle sheds.

Kerosene lamps were still used. Kerosene lanterns were used by the men folks to possum hunt and to finish up around the barn.

We were still going to the one-room school. We had one teacher for the six grades with an average of 20 to 26 pupils.

Dr. Bob Walker still served the community as the doctor to deliver babies and treat diseases.

We had two country stores in the community where we bought the necessary items that we didn't raise on the farm.

The mail was delivered to the rural route six times a week. Postage for a letter was 2 cents and a post card 1 cent.

Just before daylight the men folks were out feeding the livestock and the pigs. They would be getting ready to face a hard day of work on the farm.

This was still the time when every weed was cut from the field of corn. The tobacco was wormed, suckered, and cut by hand. Then it was classed into five classes and ready for the earliest market. This was the only source of money for the tenant farmer.

In the winter months before Wiley went to the barn to feed the livestock he built fires in the fireplace and the wood cook stove.

When the hay was cut, the hayloft was filled and there would be stacks of hay also. The hay was pitched to the hayloft with a pitchfork.

Corn was stored in the corncrib until every Friday night some was shelled to take to the corn mill for making corn meal. A portion of the meal was traded to the miller for grinding the turn of corn. Livestock and pigs were fed the nubbins.

Cutting corn was still done by hand. First the ear of corn was removed then, the fodder was pulled. That would be fed to the livestock. The stalks would be hauled away to a poor section of the land and left there. Sometimes there would not be enough time, then the corn was cut and the stalks with the corn was shocked until time to work it up.

Sometime after this the choppers were put to work and the corn shucker that was operated by a tractor would shuck the corn. Then there were silos for storing the chopped feed. Things were beginning to change.

All the winter wood was cut, logged off the mountain and then pulled to the wood yard by the horses. The logs were cut in sections with a crosscut saw and the wood was chopped with an axe. All was still done by hand.

Winter months the farmers would take time to make tobacco sticks from wood to hang the tobacco on. The fences now were made with wooden fence stakes and barbwire.

The handles for the axes, hammers, and other tools were still handmade from wood.

Tenant homes were still not warm. They were still heated with wood. The openness of the house and no insulation kept the house from getting warm.

My family, 1924. Flora Kinsland and Ruth Kinsland. 1930, Dollie, Louise, Flora, and Mazie (Wiley in Background). 1929, Louise. Styles from these early days

Back Row: Ruth, Louise, Flora, Mazie
Front Row: Beatrice, Fannie, Garrett Jr. Kinsland

Left: Fannie   Right: Flora, Garrett Jr. and Beatrice.

Old wash pot in back ground of right picture.

What was it like in kitchens gone by? Kerosene lamp, coffee grinder, pie pans, canning jars, dish pans for washing dishes.

Cornshocks are of the past.

Old black iron cooking pans and water kettle used in fireplace.

Donated photo by Katherine Wells Jackson

Top: Enamel coffee pot, lantern, water dipper
Left: Pie safe
Right: Gourd dipper

Top of an old wood cook stove showing an old iron frying pan. To the left of the pan is a stove eyehook.

Old pans, wash pan and water dipper.

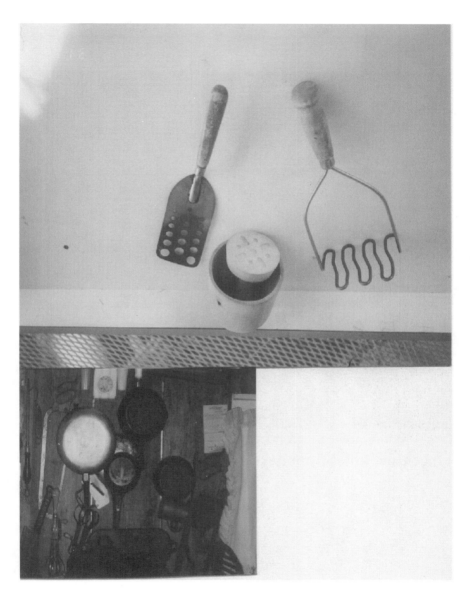

In my Grandmother's language. This is an egg turner, butter mold and a tater masher. Below: Old pans.

Once used toilet from days gone by.

Corn crib used for storing shucked corn.

Kerosene lamps, stove irons, old pans from my mother's kitchen. Things of the past, even the snuff boxes, foreground.

Richland Rolling Mill, Lake Junaluska 1939
Top: Francis Mill – Francis Cove

This old hog pen had been deserted in 1989 when this picture was taken. Since then it has fallen. In the pasture around the hog pen were the farmer's cattle. There is a stream of water in foreground.

Above: Cabbage cutter used in making kraut. Old sausage grinder.
Lower: Sausage frying in balls to be canned.

When sausage was canned, it was turned up-side down so the grease would be on top when opened. The sausage grease was used in making gravy.

Everyone was allotted acres of land according to their acreage for tobacco. Tobacco was their main source of money. This is a tobacco field of 1999. Farmers still make money from tobacco sales. Barn with silo to the left.

Dishes collected from inside boxes of oatmeal by my family.

Life Was Still Rough

Life was still rough. I was young at this time and I remembered how hard my Grandpa, Wiley worked in the hot sun and how he worked feeding the livestock, classing tobacco, and just keeping enough wood to keep the fires going in the farmhouse.

My mother, Flora (daughter of Wiley and Dollie), had married Garrett Kinsland. My father had become ill when I was ten years old and my youngest sister was two months old.

When my father passed away, my mother was left with six children. One child had passed away.

There was an orphanage home that took people who needed help. Standing in the graveyard at my father's funeral, I heard some people saying, "She will have to put them in the Orphan Home."

My grandparents had two children still at home and they had taken two of Wiley's sister's children.

We moved in the house with them. This made a total of thirteen. The crowded house was clean but very cold. It was home and this is where we learned to share, love, to work, to cope with life, and we survived.

We learned all the things that we must do like: carrying in water, feeding the chickens, bringing the cows in at milking time, working in the fields, churning the milk, walking wherever we went, bringing in the wood, and helping take care of our younger brother and sisters.

We still had to use the outside toilet, take baths in the kitchen by the heated stove, wash clothes with the scrub boards, and iron with the heavy irons that had been heated in the fireplace or on top of the wood cook stove.

We did have something new on the cook stove. We had a reservoir to heat water. This helped in washing the dishes and getting baths. Winter months we carried water to fill the washtubs for heating on the cook stove.

This was necessary for washing clothes.

We children spent a lot of time around the cook stove for warmth while we studied our school lessons. We used the kerosene lamp on the kitchen table for light.

We enjoyed coming home from school to find sausage balls, baked sweet potatoes or Irish potatoes in the warmer on the cook stove. There might be pots of vegetables pushed back on the stove, also. Our school lunches had been jelly and biscuits or cornbread and milk carried in a pint jar. Winter months the teacher cooked various kinds of soups and stews on top of the pot-bellied stove.

We were still using Octagon soap and homemade lye soap for washing clothes. We had Lifebuoy soap for bathing. We had toothbrushes that had been given to each child at the school. When our toothbrushes wore out we had toothbrushes from birch wood.

Without electricity we had no conveniences. But we did have a battery radio. The battery was saved, so we thought, by not using it too much. When it needed charging, it had to be carried to town. The batteries were large.

We had programs that we listened to. The adults listened to the weather and the news.

Our haircuts were all done at home. We children had haircuts by a neighbor woman. The men gathered around the fire or under the shade trees to get their haircuts. They used a straight razor for shaving. To sharpen the razor they used a leather strap.

Feathers would be removed from the pillow and bed ticks, so the ticks could be washed.

The house was completely cleaned. The cooking utensils were taken to the branch bank and scrubbed with sand to remove the build up of the black from them.

The women folks canned everything they could to help with the winter supply of food. Our cellars were full of filled cans. There were potatoes and cabbage stored for winter use. Sweet potatoes were rolled in newspaper to keep for the winter.

By now we had a store on wheels that delivered a lot more things that we could not get at the country store. They also took chickens and eggs as trade-ins for merchandise needed.

Wiley and Dollie's children had all married and gone away. This left the grandchildren to help with more things since the boys in the family had moved.

We had collected a set of dishes, measuring cups, measuring spoons, and milk glass glasses from the purchase of oatmeal. In the large boxes you would find plates, bowls and large items. In the small boxes you would find the smaller items. We were really proud of this collection.

Our cupboards and safes looked much better with these dishes that we used only on Sundays or when company came.

There were still a lot of homemade medicines. There was also Castor Oil, Liniments, Epsom Salt, and a few others.

Grandpa still followed the signs in planting the crops and grubbing up the excess briars and bushes. He said if you followed the signs then this would kill the briars and bushes and he didn't have to do this as often. He watched the sky, the sun, and the moon to tell what the weather would be. Since he could neither read nor write, by telling the position of the sun he knew what time of day it was.

There was very little mail. As soon as Grandma received a letter from her brother in Knoxville, Tennessee, it was answered. Since Grandma could neither read nor write she had one of the grandchildren write her letter. She told us the words to write. We had received a little more education so we were able to write better letters for Grandma. We omitted a lot of the things she told us and wrote it in our own words.

One of the neighbors, Mrs. Mandy Sanford received a Home Comfort Magazine. In the magazine there was an order blank to order impression material for making false teeth. She asked another neighbor, Mrs. Ethel McCracken if she would make the impression so she could mail it back to receive the teeth. It worked out great. The teeth fit perfectly and she wore them until her death. Mail was very important. There was no junk mail.

The men were getting out sawmill wood for the Champion Plant in their spare time. This gave them extra money. They were also trapping for hides of many animals that would be sold. Ginseng roots were collected to sell also.

Changes were somewhat better since the men folks had a little more money. Some of them had cars. The roads were still routed out. They were almost impossible to travel with the rainy and snowy conditions.

The convicts were taking care of the roads. They carried their food for cooking. The guard carried a gun and he watched them closely. However, sometimes they got away and then they brought bloodhounds to search for them.

The community women would reward them for a job well done by cooking a meal for them.

All this certainly has changed.

Sheep raised by Bill Buchanan. Picture taken 1999.

Collection of kitchen utensils from Mama's and Grandma's kitchen: jug, pie plates, spoon holder, and glass ware.

Collection of items from my Mama's and Grandma's kitchen: Milk jar, canning jars, handmade dough roller, butter mold and coffee grinder.

Old wash pot used for boiling
clothes
by Katherine Wells Jackson.

Below: Scrub board or wash
board
by Katherine Wells Jackson.

Sometimes the clothesline would be full and the barb-wire fences would also be full. Clothes you would see blowing in the wind were Long Johns (Men's long underwear) and overalls.

Wash Days:　Come Monday morning the clothes were rubbed out on the washboard.　All the women folks tried to be the first to get the clothes on the line.　They depended on the sun for drying.

Aprons: A must for all the womenfolks. Aprons had many uses.

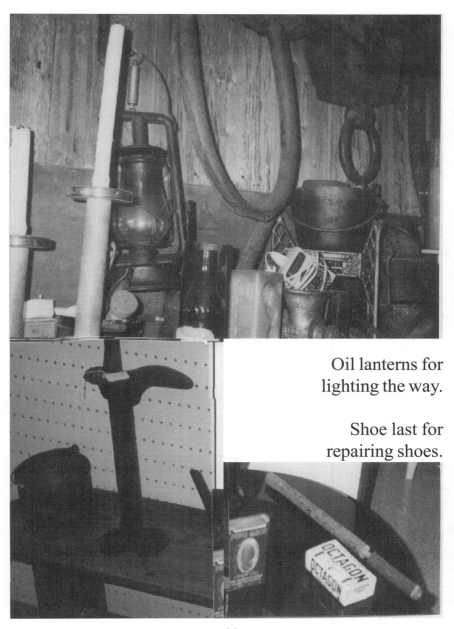

Oil lanterns for lighting the way.

Shoe last for repairing shoes.

Above:
Corn patch-Bald Creek
1998

Corn planter

Donated photo

Horse drawn hay rake.

Top: Cob crusher   donated picture

Bottom: One horse hill side plow

Old farm equipment from Kelly's farm at Big Branch. Old planter found in a flea market in Georgia.

Animal hides were a means of earning extra money for the men folks.

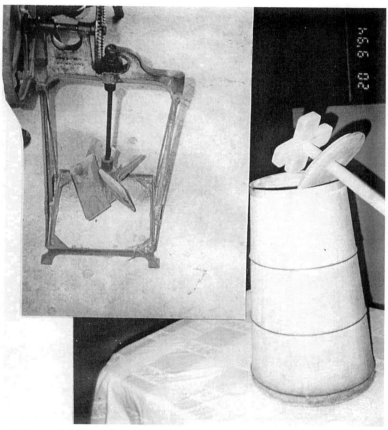

Top: First old crank type churn- the bowl sat in the bottom.
Bottom: The churn that became so popular for many years.
The dash was pushed up and down until the butter formed.

The butter mold was used to press the print of butter after churning the milk.

The old crock jar was used to hold the sweet milk that would clabber. Later it was used as a churn. The clabbered milk was churned into butter and buttermilk.
Left: Old dresser.

More Changes In The Late 1930's

We had a new school now. The one-room school had been sold and there would not be another one-room school in our community.

The first thing we noticed was the different style of clothes that the children wore.

We had been picking and selling blackberries for 5cents a gallon. We had picked beans for the landlord also. With the money from these beans we had bought material, buttons, patterns and thread to make three dresses and a skirt and blouse. Mama (Flora Kinsland) had bought each of us some anklets (socks). All our dresses had not been made yet. There were still times that we had to wear the feed and flour sack dresses. The girls at school made fun of us and we were very uncomfortable. Soon our dresses were complete. But we still had a problem. The hairstyles had changed.

We were still picking beans and tomatoes for the landlord and we had a little money. As soon as we had enough we went to town with him. His plans were to stay all day. This would give us time to get a permanent wave in our hair. Other children had them and they had beautiful curls.

We were afraid of all the electric curlers that would be connected to our hair. What if a lightning storm came? We lived through it. This certainly was a change from curling our hair with strips torn from paper pokes (bags).

Everything changed and we did well until cold weather came. Mama knew we needed the long, dark colored stockings to keep us warm. This didn't work. The girls made fun of us again. Until our mother could get money for buying socks, we were required to wear them.

Shoes (slippers) were better now. They lasted longer and the shoes were repaired at the shoe stores after this.

A very frightening machine to us girls who were going to get their first permanent wave (to make their hair curly). All these clamps were connected to the hair and then the electricity was turned on.

Blackberries would be sold for .05¢ a gallon.

Farm equipment was changing with each year. The farm now had tractors. The mules and horses were still used, also. The tractor was used to pull the molasses machine.

In heating the house we now had a wood heater. This was a cleaner heat and it was a better heat.

Tin roofs had replaced the handmade shingle roofs. We enjoyed listening to the rain dripping on the tin roof when we retired to the upstairs.

Poison sprays had to be used to kill the insects that were destroying the crops. Fertilizers were used to help produce more crops.

In the early 1940s electricity came to the rural community. We had a light bulb hanging down from the middle of each room. What a great light!

The first thing we bought was an electric iron. It was a pleasure to iron.

Most all the cloth was still cotton and had been starched with a paste of flour and water. Boxes of dry starch came later. There was a socket that screwed into the light outlet, and then the iron and eventually the radio was plugged into this socket. There were no wall outlets yet. We looked in the Sears & Roebuck catalog at the new appliances that might be ours someday. Mama and Grandma still prepared a big dinner on Sundays.

We looked forward to our company, which were aunts, uncles, and cousins. The dishes all had to be done by hand. There was no indoor plumbing. Water was still carried from the spring.

We were very much behind in our schoolwork that first year. We had not heard of a lot of things in Geography and History.

We had been lucky in the one-room school that we hadn't got the lice and itch. No one had it in our school. In the new school we got both of them the first year.

Grandpa, Grandma, and Mama decided to move farther into the country, still on one of the McCrary's farms. Life was becoming harder for Grandpa to keep up the farm work. We then moved to smaller farm, the Homer Trantham farm. This is where I found a job one day a week in the Country Store. Wages weren't much. We were taught typing, Home Economics, and other subjects. This was a different world.

In the meantime, The Home Extension Of Haywood County introduced the art of making mattresses at the school. We girls went to the school with our mother and we made three. The cost of the material was $11.00 each.

This eliminated some of the feather beds, which were too soft. This was a great improvement.

As soon as my sister and I graduated from school, we rode the work bus to Waynesville to work in the factory. Soon we married and each had a child.

Since there was not much for Mama to do on the smaller farm we persuaded her to move with us. She brought our younger sister and brother with her.

Our brother then went to the Armed Service and our sister had a better chance in graduation from a larger school.

Eventually we persuaded Grandpa and Grandma to move to town with us. Grandpa was not young enough to keep up farm work.

My husband, Floyd Nelson, from my second marriage, and I built them a home. Mama had learned all the new electric appliances. Having oil heat and having means of traveling in a car was new for them.

Grandma and Grandpa had not advanced much. They had the small light bulb for light, an iron and a radio. That was as far as they got.

By now the whole country had changed. People had moved away from the farms to work in factories. The ones still living on the farm were buying meal, flour, eggs, shortening, sugar, coffee, milk, and almost everything from the super food store.

There was no need for animals any more on the farm. The animal buildings were falling to the ground. The corn mills had closed. The tractors were doing the work that the horses and mules once did. Horses were becoming pleasure horses. There were power saws to get the wood cut.

There were very few milk cows left. The berries and nuts had been sprayed and killed to get the pastures cleared. They were fast being destroyed. The ducks were not needed for featherbeds and pillows. You could buy all the clothes from the department stores. Whatever was needed, it was in the major stores. Farms were fading away as for dependences of living.

Chickens stayed on foot until time to have fried chicken or chicken and dumplings, most of the time on Sunday. From the Kelly Farm – Big Branch.

Mother hens trained the chicks to find food by scratching up the soil and clucking to them.

You would find hen's nest on the side of the chicken house.

Eggs

Molasses Making at Big Branch-The Kelly Farm

Times changed from when the mules or horses pulled the pole around to operate the molasses mill. Now days the engine does the work and the tractor hauls away the cane stalks to cover bare spots on the fields.

Courtesy of Bill Buchanan
This picture was taken 1999. Notice snow on the ground.
The barbwire fence and split wood is still used now days.

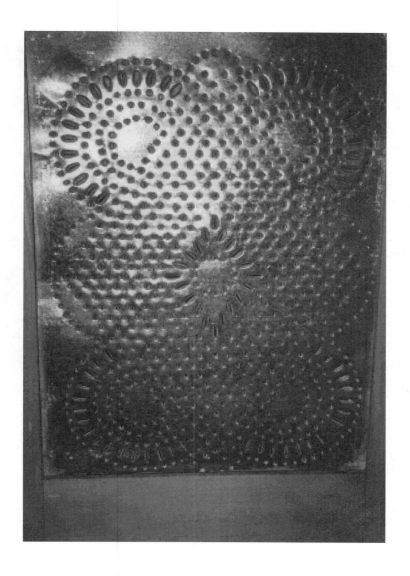

A door of a safe or a cupboard from the old days.

Old kitchen cupboard – bowl of eggs. This was when the white kitchen cabinets became popular.

Collection of items by my family; each oatmeal box contained some of these.

Many women folks still do canning.

Display by Mrs. Jim Parker: Dried apples, apple pie, canned apples, sifter, and handmade dough roller made by Garrett Kinsland (my father). Dough roller is over 100 years old.

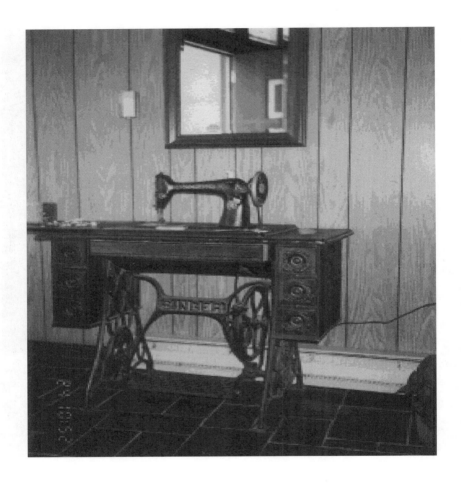

The old pedaled sewing machine. Used by all the women folks to make the feed and flour sack dresses, curtains, quilt linings and etc.

This quilt was made by my Mama, Flora Kinsland, in 1980. She still used the old quilting frames. To hold the lining, filling and quilt top together in the frames, shoe tacks were used. First quilts were made out of necessity.

Pleasure quilts by mother in later years.

The girls were taught to spin yarn on the spinning wheel. They learned to knit using the yarn. They were taught to use the pedal sewing machine to make their clothes. Dresser scarves were embroidered.

Milking dairy cows changed
over the years from being
milked by hand to being
milked by a machine. Milk
was stored in the milk cans
and sit by the side of the road,
 waiting to be picked up
by the milk truck to be
delivered to the dairies.

The farmers had beehives and there were times they would find a bee swarm. They would get honey from the hollow trees where the bees made the honey.

Photo donated by Benton McCrary

Wiley Caldwell, My grandfather and his landlord; Bill McCrary.

A Farm Of Yesterday

Nestled in the cove of Big Branch, Jerry Massie lived with his mother in a one-room log cabin.

Jerry's father had been killed when he was visiting the Harley Seay's home by lightning. They lived in a log cabin.

Jerry and his mother eventually built a farmhouse and turned the log cabin into a smokehouse.

Jerry married, and he and his wife, Arby Massie lived with their 12 children in the beautiful farmhouse.

Two of Uncle Jerry and Aunt Arby's grandchildren, Charlie Massie and Earl Massie took these pictures of the Massie home in February 1995. Mr. and Mrs. Charlie Nolan of Greensboro, N. C. owned this farm at this time. With their permission I will use this story of how the newly farmhouses came into being after the old log cabins were gone.

No one seems to know what year it was built. When I lived with my grandparents in the Big Branch community, in the late 1920s, this house was there. The McCrary farm that we lived on was next to this farm.

These first old log cabins that we both lived in were possibly among the first to be built in the Big Branch community.

Uncle Jerry passed away in 1948. He was possibly in his mid 80s. This might help to determine the age of the farmhouse.

117

Most of the house was built of logs with mud. The chimney is rocks and mud. The farmhouse had graduated from a shingle roof to a tin roof.

The upstairs of the house was bedrooms. Aunt Arby's kitchen was on the back. I remember going to the kitchen to get milk and butter when our cows were dry. All neighbors saw that every one had milk when the cows were dry. Everyone shared.

At the left of the house was a cave like section where the family went during storms.

Down the right side of the house were the remains of a rock wall that had been cleared from the fields. A footbridge crosses the branch that flows from the many springs on the farm. The family outside toilet still stands.

Around the farm are many buildings, including an old hog pen, remains of the covered spring, and a fallen shed, which was possibly a tobacco shed- structure once common to farms in these parts. There's an old barn still standing on the land. Behind it looms Chamber's Mountain.

The farm in this cove was once a good farming section. They grew everything they needed for the family needs. There were cattle in the pasture, hogs in the lots, chickens in the yard and in the henhouse. On the side of the buildings were hen nests for the chickens. Ducks were swimming in the branch, ready to have the feathers plucked for pillows and featherbeds. The boys trapped the branches for animals to be used for hides.

The tobacco was grown so there would be tobacco money for the family's salaries.

Another thing of the past, every older person was addressed as "Uncle or Aunt" or "Mr. and Mrs."

A very lovely old home of Jerry Massie at Big Branch. Rock building in back was perhaps a can house.

Old barn with a shed for the milk cow or to hang cut tobacco in.

The old hog pen from many years ago.

A covered spring that supplied all the water for the Massie's large family.

Donated Photo
Charlie Massie & Pauline Massie
Foot log leading to the outside toilet and the hog pen.

A Brief Description Of Some Changes

Postal Service

Postage is another ways of changes. The postal cards begin in 1863 with 1 cent and in the year 1991 it was 19 cents. Letters began this same year 2 cents to 33 cents in 2000.

1775-1993

Domestic Rates For Letters And Postcards

Prior to the middle of the 19th century, rates were based on the number of sheets in a letter and the distance it was traveling. In 1845, rates were based on the weight of a letter and the distance it was going. Beginning in 1863, domestic letters rates became "uniform," that is, they were based solely on weight, regardless of distance.

Postage listed below is in cents.

Effective Date	Per ½ ounce
March 3, 1863	3
March 3, 1883	2
	Per Ounce
July 1, 1885	2
November 3, 1917	3
July 1, 1919	2
July 6, 1932	3
August 1, 1958	4

Postage listed below is in cents. Continued...

January 7, 1963	5
January 7, 1968	6
May 16, 1971	8
March 2, 1974	10

Each

	First Ounce	Additional Ounce
September 14, 1975	10	9
December 31, 1975	13	11
May 29, 1978	15	13
March 22, 1981	18	17
November 1, 1981	20	17
February 17, 1985	22	17
April 3, 1988	25	20
February 3, 1991	29	23

Postal cards (Postal Service Issued) and Postcards (Privately Mfg.)

Effective date	Postal Cards	Postcards
May 1, 1873	1	—
July 1, 1898	1	1
November 3, 1917	2	2
July 1, 1919	1	1
April 15, 1925	1	2
July 1, 1928	1	1
January 1, 1952	2	2
August 1, 1958	3	3

January 7, 1963	4	4
January 7, 1968	5	5
May 16, 1971	6	6
September 14, 1975	7	7
December 31, 1975	9	9
May 29, 1978	10	10
March 22, 1981	12	12
November 1, 1981	13	13
February 17, 1985	14	14
April 3, 1988	15	15
February 3, 1991	19	19

Mail carrying has changed also. Mail was delivered in towns by horseback and stagecoach. Then it came by car delivery and walkers. There are mail delivery trucks now. Or you might want your mail delivered to the Post Office where you have a box. Post Offices have changed from small buildings that were also used for other things to modern buildings.

Some of the first mail came by boats. A passenger delivered the first mail and in return was sent back by passengers.

The rural Postmaster years in the Crabtree section where I lived came to the Crabtree Post Office. Fines Creek and Ironduff picked their mail up here. It was delivered from Waynesville, N. C. There would be an average of 8 to 10 letters twice a week.

Mrs. Cumi Ferguson was the first Post Mistresses.

Little "Dock Messer," a fine horseman, delivered the mail on horseback to the home of Dr. Bill Ferguson. He received 10 cents a day for his wages. In 1908, Coman Francis carried the mail by horse and cart to the rural routes.

Another Post Office was at Huggensville, (now known as Bald Creek). Fate McCracken was the postmaster with George Rogers as the first rural mail carrier by horse.

In the 1930s, Coman Francis delivered the mail by car. The mail was delivered from the Clyde, N. C. Post Office.

The roads were in bad shape so there was a row of mailboxes at the entrance of every side road.

Time was involved and this saved a few hours for every one to pick up the mail at the entrance of each road. The trip was very long to Fines Creek, Crabtree and Hyder Mountain.

Everyone knew what time to expect the mailman. They needed to wait for him if they wanted to mail a package or to get stamps.

The mailman would tell if there had been an accident, marriage or death near by.

Because he was special he was given vegetables from the garden, maybe country ham or a mess of meat from a freshly killed hog. Or maybe he would receive milk or butter.

Mail is still delivered to the rural areas by car.

Postage and mail service is just one of the many changes.

THE CRABTREE POST OFFICE in the early 1900s was run by Mr. and Mrs. Claude Williams. The mail apparently was delivered in a Model

AN EARLIER Post Office in Crabtree was located in a store operated by Eli and Cumi Ferguson and was called "Ferguson." The mail carriers standing beside the mail buggy are Jeter Hawkins left and Grady Worley.

Medical Services

I suppose this has been one of the major changes in history. The early pioneers had homemade medicine. Everyone did what he or she could do when someone was sick. The midwives delivered the babies.

Then there were the community doctors. Most of them operated from their homes or had a very small office.

In the community where we lived, Dr. Bob Walker was the doctor. He first came to the home in a buggy or by horseback. If it was late or if someone was very sick then he spent the night and days if needed. He delivered all the babies in the community. Each of my siblings and I were delivered at home. Sometimes he didn't arrive in time and the neighbor women would deliver the babies. Dr. Walker had an office in his home. This was the living room, which was called the front room.

Waynesville and Canton had several doctors that began services in the towns. Each town now had a small hospital. Doctor offices and hospitals changed in size. They now have all the conveniences. They are well staffed with nurses and with doctors for every type of illnesses.

The modern ways of doing the services and the modern up to date equipment keeps changing for the better.

Of course with the changes the price increase of services had to change also.

Some of the sample prices of service and the time

spent in the hospital were like this:

The Waynesville Hospital 1923

Appendicitis	10 days	22.00
Gunshot wound	8 days	31.00
Tonsillectomy	2 days	$9.00
Pneumonia & Hernia	3 days	21.00
Burns	31 days	122.00
Broken leg	2 days	4.00
Fractured Skull	33 days	93.60
Chicken Pox	8 days	26.00
Amputation of toes	15 days	54.50

Some of the country doctors were paid in vegetables, country ham or meat. This was great for them since they had no time to make a garden or raise a hog for meat.

One of the examples that I know of was; there was an epidemic of diphtheria. One of my daddy's (Garrett Kinsland) children, by a first marriage, passed away in South Carolina. My daddy brought the body of the 5 year old in the back seat of a car to Haywood County to be buried. With no communication, there was no way to let him know that another child had passed away, with the same disease, and was buried in South Carolina.

All the coffins, (caskets) were made at home. A member of the family or friends dug the graves by hand.

Caskets were later sold at the furniture stores. Then the embalming service began. The funeral homes were small to begin with and now they are modern. The funeral service, with visitation and keeping of the body is taken care of by the Funeral Home. Employees from the Funeral Home are in charge of the grave digging, which is done by machines.

Today in the year 2000, funeral services are taken care of by the Funeral Homes. For a complete medical history try Heritage Of Healing by Nina and William Anderson.

Waynesville Hospital, Pigeon Street

Dr. J.H. Way's office. Built 1889.

Office of Dr. J. F. Abel. Main Street. Waynesville

Robert Lee Walker

Robert Lee Walker, son of Spencer and Nancy Hyatt Walker, was born February 15, 1865, in the Crabtree community of Haywood County. Spencer Walker apparently had some involvement with medicine as well as law and in 1863 had been chairman of the committee which drafted the law to prevent the spread of smallpox. Robert Walker's obituary stated that he began practicing medicine at the age of seventeen, which would have been in 1881; presumably he was studying with and assisting one of the local Crabtree physicians, possibly one of the Drs. Roberts. He earned a medical degree from the Kentucky School of Medicine in Louisville in 1889. His name appears on the roll of honor for his class.

Dr. Walker began his medical practice in Clyde, where Dr. Charles Roberts was then practicing, and later relocated to Crabtree. From 1889 to 1891 he served as county coroner. Dr. Walker dealt with common problems and saw serious outbreaks of typhoid, smallpox and pneumonia. He never had an office but saw patients at his home, where he also mixed his own medicines. Beginning as a "horse and buggy" doctor, in later years Dr. Walker continued to attend patients even though he never purchased an automobile or learned to drive. Patients would get Dr. Walker, either bringing him home or keeping him overnight as a guest.

At his death on June 28, 1944, Dr. Walker was described as a "practicing physician for 51 years." The announcement stated that Dr. Walker "at the time of his last illness, he was visiting some of his patients in Madison County and the Gulf section of Tennessee." Dr. Walker is buried in the Crabtree Baptist Church Cemetery.

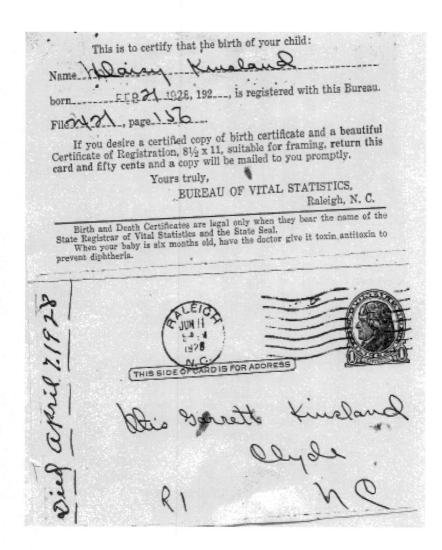

This is to certify that the birth of your child:

Name _____

born _____ FEB 21 1928, 192____, is registered with this Bureau.

Filed _____, page _____.

If you desire a certified copy of birth certificate and a beautiful Certificate of Registration, 8½ x 11, suitable for framing, return this card and fifty cents and a copy will be mailed to you promptly.

Yours truly,

BUREAU OF VITAL STATISTICS,

Raleigh, N. C.

Birth and Death Certificates are legal only when they bear the name of the State Registrar of Vital Statistics and the State Seal.
When your baby is six months old, have the doctor give it toxin antitoxin to prevent diphtheria.

Children's births were registered in Raleigh, North Carolina. Birth date was February, card received June, child died April, and post card was 1 cent. There are many changes from this time.

Champion Hospital Canton

Electric Services

To me the greatest invention has been electricity. So many things are controlled by electricity. It is impossible to tell the changes that electricity makes in the world. The changes are many per day. The way of living in the world was so undeveloped and so hard to cope with before electricity.

Towns in this area began with electricity in 1908. In the country electricity began in the 1930s. In the part of the country where I lived, it began 1942.

This changed everything for the better.

This is an electric bill In Waynesville in the year 1937.

TOWN OF WAYNESVILLE
LIGHT AND WATER DEPARTMENT

BILLS PAYABLE BETWEEN 1st AND 10th.

Readings		Used		Amount		Unpaid Balance	Total Due	Date
Present	Previous	Current	Water	Current	Water			
MIN				1.20	1.10		2.30	MAY 1 37

Minimum Light, 15 K. W. H. or less $1.20; Water $1.10

J R GERRNGER

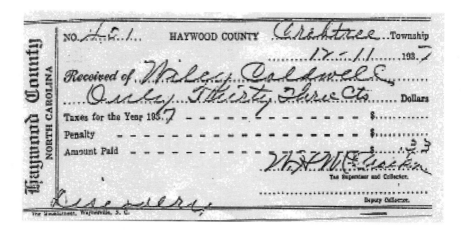

    This Tax Receipt was 12-11-1937 where my grandfather, Wiley Caldwell paid a total of 33 cents. They called it a discovery tax. My grandfather owned no land, no car and no electric appliances, because electricity had not come to the rural area.

    The tax collector's office sent someone into the rural areas to collect taxes.

    My grandfather, Wiley Caldwell owned a dog which he might have paid taxes on.

Heating

The first Haywood County homes were heated with wood burning in the fireplace. As time went on there was a heater with burning wood, which was an easier way of heating. Then there was coal. Coal could be bought by the truck or by the toe-sack. Eventually there were the heaters and furnaces for the home that was controlled by oil. Furnaces had changed from the coal to the oil. There was also steam heat, using hot water. Then the most important heat came about. It was electric. However, some people still enjoy the fireplace with the wood or the new modern wood stoves. Fireplaces are heated with gas. This is very important. There has to be means of heating when the electricity is off. Gas and wood are still used for that.

Heater from days gone by.

Clothing

Clothing has certainly come a long ways. It began with leather, homespun wool and then cotton. After this, many types of material were bought.

Clothing was still simple when I was growing up. There were the feed and flour sacks that made not only our dresses, but also our underwear. Sheets, towels, washcloths, quilt linings and other things were made from the heavier feed sacks. Then the flannel material became popular to make quilt linings.

Clothes were very hard to iron. Cotton material was the worst. The starching of the material didn't help any. Neither did the irons that were heated on the wood cook stove or in the fireplace, because they didn't hold heat long.

The starch was made from flour and water that was heated together and then strained in a flour sack.

Other things that the flour sacks were good for was to strain berry juice in making jellies. They were used to strain milk when the milking of the cows was done. Still another thing was to store beans, corn and vegetable seeds for next years crop. They were used to store dried vegetables and fruits. The loft over our kitchen had many things hanging in flour sacks. Finally the flour and feed sack days were over and material could be bought from 5 cents to 15 cents a yard.

The women folks had a pedal sewing machine. This was great for making clothes. All the power that was needed was the muscle of the foot and leg.

Today, hardly any one makes clothes, even though there are electric sewing machines.

It is much easier to buy any piece of clothing you need from the many large department stores. This includes any type of material and most doesn't have to be ironed.

The styles have changed many times over the last 120 years. Anything seems to be the style now days.

Shoes have changed a lot over the years. The first shoes were handmade. The men's shoes were called brogans. One person that I have heard of that made the brogan shoes in Ratcliff Cove-Waynesville, N.C. was Bill Gaddy, Tom Gaddy's son. One of the helpers was Bob Underwood.

The brogan shoes were made good but the women and children's shoes were sown together with thread that didn't hold. The soles were forever tearing apart and had to be repaired at home on a shoe last with shoe tacks.

The first shoemakers and repairmen were called cobblers. There are shoe repair shops now. Shoes are not repaired as much as they once were. In most cases it is cheaper to invest in buying another pair of shoes. Again there are large shoe stores and they can be bought in many styles. This year 2000, almost any style is in.

Water Means Of Haywood County

Haywood County is well blessed by the many streams, branches, creeks and springs.

For many years the water supply was from springs. Then wells were dug and each city has their own water system, with a bountiful supply of the cleanest, purest water.

More water is used now than ever was. The livestock has plenty of water. In W. Clark Medford Haywood County Books, he states that we have 2500 named branches, streams and brooks. There are many unnamed. Each of the springs, brooks, streams, branches and creeks travel down the mountainsides to form large branches. The Pigeon River originated in the Pisgah community. Then the water flows until it becomes the Pigeon River.

This gives an idea as how well the Pigeon River is watered. Pigeon River's name is believed to have come from the many pigeons that conjugated around the river.

Over the years the creeks and branches supplied the water for the gristmills.

There are many things that depend on the water supplies.

The big change was the watershed that holds enough water to supply the towns and part of the county.

Travel

Travel as mentioned before began with the oxen pulling the carts and wagons. Then the horses for horse back riding, pulling the carriages, wagons and sleds.

There are boats, cars, ships, canoes, trains, small planes, and large jet planes, helicopters, bicycle, motorcycles, and space machines. There is a lot to say about traveling.

With the improvement of the roads and the improvement of the vehicles what more can be said?

Changes will be made.

145

From Oxen to Trains

Oxen were very important in carrying lumber, working the fields, pulling the sleds and wagons.

Horses were faster and traveling was a little different. Horses and mules were excellent for pulling loads, pulling carriages, buggies, sleds, and wagons. The speed of the horses made working in the fields faster. They were popular for horseback riding. Even the early white settlers could travel over the mountain terrain in locating the right spot for building their cabins and traveling the lands that they could choose for their own.

Then trains were the fast means for transporting lumber to the pulp mill at Canton, N.C.

Many men were required to help build the railroads into the mountains for the trains to deliver the lumber to the Champion Pulp Mill. This gave the men a chance to earn money for supporting their families.

Families moved into the Sunburst areas and the Cherokee areas where they acquired working with the oxen, then horses and trains for transporting lumber.

Passenger trains began arriving around the early 1800's. Until 1949 there were 7 passenger trains daily to bring the visitors into Haywood County. This was means of travel for everyone, going from section of the county to towns. Train fares from Waynesville to Clyde were 5¢.

Then personal cars came to Waynesville and Canton, N.C. There were also buses and taxis. Times improved in traveling. Then there were the jets, the helicopters and space ships to the moon.

John Norris in front of Oldsmobile dealership that he had in the 1920's. This is on Commerce St. looking North toward the intersection at Frog Level.
John married Edna Faye Miller daughter of Robert Edgar and Mary Mull Miller.

Homes

Homes began very simple. They changed from this small log cabin to larger log homes, then frames and rock. Large frame homes became popular after all the sawmills and the lumber. Brick homes began. The houses were modern with all the conveniences. Now days the outside is vinyl. Brick has become too expensive.

Barns has changed from logs and frame to the modern ones with silos. There are not a lot of barns left. The ones left are very large to accommodate the livestock of now days.

5. Moody farm log barn, upper Fines Creek, 19th century

Donated by Haywood Homes Example of a log barn, in later years frame sheds were added. Notice wooden latch on door- a very popular style of latches.

Donated photo by Ann Kinsland
Old buildings by the side of the road.

Courtesy of Haywood Homes and History
Frame homes became popular, but rock houses remained
popular from the beginning, after logs.

This is a very picturesque farm home with the slope of the mountains in background.

Shook-Smathers house, Clyde, c.1795

. Patton house, Canton vicinity, c. 1830s

Shook-Smathers house was possible the first frame house.

Patton House-is believed to be the second framed one.

Donated photo by Bob Allen
Emmett Green's rock storage shed on Dellwood Road.
Used for many things.

Very few old log barns are still standing.

Donated by Bob Allen

This old rock apple house is still standing in the Ninevah section of Haywood County. Rock was a good way to go with all the rocks that were available.

Donated photo by Bob Allen
Old barn with once used silo. This was a big change for storing food for the livestock. Located on Howell Mill Road.

Log and frame barns of the past. This one has a tin roof.

Hay harvesting has changed from the haystacks to bails
and from hay cutting to machines. Cattle are waiting for a
truck to transport them.

When baptizing was done in the creeks; it looks like many people lined up to be baptized. (Baptizing of Mrs. Howell Crawford's mother)

War Rationing Stamps

The United States Government issued rationing stamps during the war as means of getting items that had a shortage. Some of the items that were rationed were sugar and coffee. At a different time gasoline was rationed.

This is a War Ration Book with the stamps that belonged to Mrs. Bird Nelson. Mrs. Nelson is the mother of my husband, Floyd Nelson.

Another interesting thing was that three of Mrs. Nelson's and her husband's sons left for the armed service the same day.

The United States Government works out the necessary things as they arise.

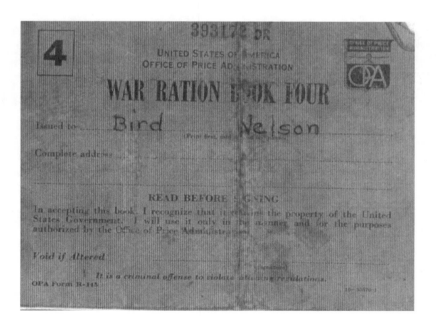

Early Town Years

Early Town Years
1790-1943
Waynesville, N.C.

There had to be a starting point. All towns and countries started in the same way.

I have chosen to tell how Waynesville, N.C. began.

Many people have told me bits and pieces of Waynesville and I am using W. Clark Medford's Haywood County History Books. Mr. Medford spent many years in capturing the early history of Haywood County and Waynesville, N.C. In fact, a lot of people would say, "That's the way Mr. Medford explains it."

I give Mr. Medford credit for information in this chapter.

Check my latest book, "Historic Waynesville & Haywood County," for description and pictures.

Early settlers moved into Haywood County in 1785. My husband's ancestor, David Nelson, was among this first group to move to Haywood County.

Col. Robert Love, along with 25 other people, settled in Mount Prospect. There were fifteen homes.

Most of the early settlers were from the Revolutionary War.

The soldiers were given land. All they had to do was claim the land and start a dwelling. They registered it in the Entry book in Waynesville, N.C..

For the next few years they were busy deciding what land they wanted and staked it off for theirs.

They came with the bare necessities as; oxen, or some of them a horse, an oxcart, clothing, food, seeds to begin the next season, some tools, cooking utensils, gun and gun powder and they brought a Bible.

Mount Prospect was a wilderness and there were wild animals.

The Indians had been moved out in 1776 by General Griffin Rutherford and 2000 soldiers.

The town became Waynesville in 1810 changing its name from Mount Prospect.

Haywood County was separated from Buncombe County 1808.

Until this time all the things that required settling by court or law was done in Buncombe County.

Like the County, they too did all their doctoring and delivering babies.

The dwellings in Waynesville and adjacent areas all had a fenced in spot for their livestock, a pen for the hogs, a house for the chickens, a garden spot and farming land to have corn for the livestock.

Like the early years in the country they first had a light by burning a knot of pine that was full of rosin.

They had welled up springs for water with a springhouse to store milk, butter and items that needed to be kept cool.

They grew everything they needed for food.

Rocks and logs were popular for the building of houses, toilets, and necessary surrounding buildings.

This continued for a few years. More people moved in the area both town and country.

Then it started changing. Some homes in the area had become boarding houses and served meals. The meals were 25 cents each.

Better homes were being built. Schools had begun. Businesses had opened up: hotels, restaurants, a court house, jail, mercantile store, hardware, a bank, harness and leather shops, barber shop, meat market, newspaper company, clothing and furniture stores, blacksmith, tanneries and a tobacco warehouse.

They had started growing tobacco to sell and Waynesville had a tobacco warehouse. There was also a shop that made wagons.

There were doctors, lawyers and dentists.

The town now had several hotels. Railroad tracks had been built and the train arrived 1884.

There were buggies as early as 1870. The horse and buggies met the visitors coming to stay at the hotels.

J.P. Swift Company had installed a few telephones by 1894. More lines were installed by 1900. The switchboard could only carry 100 lines. The office was over the McCracken Clothing Store on Main Street. Later this office was in the Doctor Rogers Building. There were two long distances lines. One of the lines was at the Reeves Drugstore and the other one was at the Waynesville Pharmacy. The monthly rate was $1.50 private lines and $2.00 party lines. The switchboard operator was paid $20.00 a month.

To produce lights in 1899, there was a battery-powered system for the ones that could afford it. The system was forever going out. Some of the homes and businesses still had kerosene lights.

There was then a very weak electric system and in 1930s electricity came to town.

With the electricity more businesses began. There was now a new Courthouse and a new jail. There was a new Hospital on N. Main Street. There were more and better schools, more banks, more churches, gift shops, shoe repair shops, along with the new modern motels.

By the late 1930s and early 1940s there were more and more new businesses. There were more industry plants like: Tannery, Lea, Dayton Rubber, Wellco, Champion and others. Enka had a large plant. This produced more employment.

There was a good Library, taxis, more individual cars, Trailway buses, theatres and Waynesville was really growing.

The street adjacent to Waynesville called Depot Street had increased their businesses. They were all doing well.

The towns near by: Clyde, Sylva, Hazelwood and Canton had many successful businesses.

Town certainly had changed. This covers many subjects on changes.

When the early town needed a jail and courthouse, the people were taxed on their land and a lot of them lost it.

By now so many people were beginning to acquire employment and the farms were beginning to suffer for help.

This brings the year up until 1943. Electricity has been credited for many of these changes.

Town's Early Boarding Houses

The boarding houses continued somewhat after the years of 1943. What was it like to have an early boarding house?

When the trains were delivering the visitors to the boarding houses and the hotels this was the time without electricity, without inside baths, using an outside toilet, heating with a fireplace and cooking on the wood cook stove.

168

There still were the cows, hogs, chickens, the gardens, chopping wood, and preparing the meals that sold for 25 cents per meal. Plus someone had to wash the linens, milk the cows and churn the butter. Either they had a big family or they had to hire help.

In W. Clark Medford's History Books Of Haywood County and Waynesville he gives the description of the gardens, the cow lot, the hog pen, and the chicken house in the back of Mrs. Emma Willis Boarding House.

He explains that Mrs. Felmet had a large yard in front of her boarding house.

He also tells of the early Hotels in Waynesville and around. They too, had to meet all these needs. Some of the Hotels that he listed are: The Dunham House, The Waynesville Hotel, The Old Battery Hotel, The White Sulphur Springs Hotel, The Meat Skin Hotel, The Kenmore, The Old Windsor Hotel, Eagles Nest and The Piedmont. Some of the newer ones were: The Lefaine Hotel, The Gordon Hotel and new ones that were just being built.

WORLD FAMOUS Eagle's Nest Hotel, erected at an elevation of almost one mile above sea level, two thousand feet above Waynesville, and 1300 feet below Plott and Jones' Peaks, catered to the South's super-rich late in the last century and early in this one. The boasted of a magnificent drive of five miles up Junaluska Mountain to its summit and the hotel. Views from the hotel and drive were said to be "beyond description." One English traveler said they even surpassed Switzerland in vastness.

John D. Rockfellow visited here . Eagle's Nest Hotel was built by William Austin Mitchell, grandfather of Bill Gilliland.

Hotel Lefaine

Mrs Felmet's Boarding House

THE OLD Kenmore Hotel.

According to W. Clark Medford's books, he states there was a water shortage in Waynesville. There was not enough spring water and some had dug wells. Some water was hauled into town.

What was it like to be the boarding house owner and to be the guest? How did the guest find out about Waynesville, N. C.?

Another business of these early days was the Apple Cider Shop of Granny Mull's.

Granny Mull's Shop was across the street from where the new courthouse was built. Granny had bought the land from R.Q. McCracken in 1890s. The lot was a large lot in back of the Gingerbread and Cider Shop where she kept her cows and chickens, along with making a garden.

Her husband, Jeremiah Mull helped Granny (Mary Roger Mull) in taking care of the livestock and seeing that she had enough wood to keep the wood cook stove going to bake the gingerbread.

Granny and her husband lived in the shop. This had to be a hard way of making a living.

They sold the gingerbread and a cup of hot apple cider for 5 cents each. The lot was paid for before the allotted time with proceeds from the sale of the Apple Cider and Gingerbread.

More Changes In Town Years
1943-1950

It took a lot of changes because the new businesses and factories required people to fit all needs.

Electricity was everywhere. Telephones were getting into all the homes. However, there were still a lot of party lines.

The Industry factories had hired many people. The wages were good and more people were building homes. More people were buying cars.

The taxis' and Trailway buses were still available.

Since so many homes were being built this required carpenters, plumbers and electricians. These were all skilled people.

Roads had improved so much. Cars were better and faster. Traveling from country to town and to other states was a pleasure for every one. Every one was beginning to know how the other towns and states lived.

Schools and colleges offered the subjects that were needed to go with the changes of the time.

The new hospital was making changes all the time. There were more doctors and specialists. There were more dentists and lawyers.

There were good heating systems in the home. The homes were well insulated.

Financing the homes and cars was made easy because of the better employment.

The town had many department and shoe stores.

Appliance stores were around selling ranges, washers and refrigerators. Dryers weren't around yet.

There were many: barber shops, beauty shops, hotels, motels, a few boarding houses remained, shoe repair shops, book store, jewelry stores with jewelry repairs, insurance companies, newspaper company, cleaners, soda shops, laundries, ice plant, car salesmen, a bakery, greater new food stores, drug stores, drive in restaurants, drive in theatres, street theatres, more banks, larger churches, two dairies, (Pet & Biltmore), and at one time there were nine service stations on Main Street. This is just a few of what was in the town.

The dairies still delivered milk to your home in glass bottles. Biltmore had a special dairy bar where everyone went on Sunday afternoon to get a taste of all the new ice creams.

There were a few homes still close to Main Street. One was on Montgomery Street owned by Sally Justice, mother of Lois Gentry.

Mrs. Justice still had a fenced in pasture behind her house with her milking cow.

One of the farmers living close by was Ceaser Ferguson. Mr. Ferguson lived where the Brian Center is now. He kept the hotels and cafes supplied with vegetables, country ham, eggs, milk, and butter.

Mr. Ferguson was one of the people that didn't own a car or at least I don't think he did. He pushed the vegetables to the cafes and hotels in his wheelbarrow and sometimes in a small wagon that he pulled.

Waynesville had other people that stand out in mind that visited Waynesville each day. One was Homer Davis. Homer hung around at the Waynesville Pharmacy. Everyone looked for Homer each day. Another one was Kyfer Moody. Another person, who had an antique store in Waynesville, was Aunt Ida Mullins.

People still loved to visit town on Saturdays. Some of them had been coming once a week to do their shopping, so it continued. They would gather around the courthouse yards and on the street talking about their new car, their jobs and building a new house. Then they would visit their favorite soda shop or cafe.

Around the Farmer's Federation building in Frog Level they would gather to talk. A lot of their conversation was, "We don't have enough help on the farm. Everyone has jobs and has moved to town."

Here they talked about trying to manage the livestock and how they had quit raising hogs for meat, chickens to supply eggs, sheep to shear, and ducks to make featherbeds and pillows. They talked how the country stores were closing and the corn mills had closed. They also talked about no need for the outside buildings like toilets, springhouse, corncrib, chicken house, hog pens, and others.

They realized that the times had changed and the animals were not needed around the farm.

They had electricity, bathrooms in the house, running water, refrigerators, oil heating stoves, and electric stoves to cook on.

They had cars and it was convenient to bring the groceries home from the Super Grocery Stores.

Life was full of changes and everyone was changing with it.

Basketball team of 1940. Each with their overalls.

Changes in Lake Junaluska and Waynesville, NC.

1920s   Tenn. tag on
                              car
A gathering in front of Haywood County Courthouse in Waynesville. Lefaine Hotel
at right of Court House. Building near Lefaine Hotel was Col. Jones's office
and residence's.   This had to be a pleasure to show off this car in foreground. Lucious Welch
left with beard, Granny Reed crossing Center. Wade Hampton left of buggy wheels.

1920s

A gathering in front of Haywood County Court House in Waynesville. Lefaine Hotel at right of Court House. Building near Lefaine Hotel was Col. Jones's office and residence's. This had to be a pleasure to show off this car in forground. Lucious Welch, left with beard, Granny Reed crossing, center. Wade Hampton left of buggy wheels.

ANOTHER one from the old days, about 1890...

Red Brick Courthouse of Haywood County, the horse and buggy and people sitting on the street in chairs, something of the past. Times have certainly changed.

WAYNESVILLE was well into her decline as an attractive town in the 1940's. Only a few trees had evaded the developer's ax, and most of the buil already were decrepit.

Early Radio & Television Days

Battery radios had changed to electric radios. Howard Jones owned the Radio Shop in Waynesville. My husband, Floyd Nelson bought this established business.

This store and the Western Auto Store were where the batteries were sold for the old battery radios. The cost was $12.00.

Floyd repaired and sold the radios. I sold the 78rpm records. Most of the recordings were easy listening such as Tommy Dorsey, Glenn Miller, Mills Brothers, and etc. We were just beginning to sell country, bluegrass, and gospel. There was some early classical music.

Electricity had just got to some of the rural areas. The record player had gone from crank-up graph- a-phone to talking machine and now to electric.

The old battery radio and the heavy batteries were fading out because for a few dollars more you could have an electric radio.

Then the records changed to 45rpm and 33 1/3rpm.

The records had to be shipped from several companies. Then they consolidated into one company.

The record players were now called High Fidelity or Phonographs. Soon they were called Stereophonic due to having two speakers. This improved the sound.

Rock and Roll music was beginning to make a hit. Our first rock and roll singer was Elvis Pressley. The parents had a hard time approving of Elvis. The children saved their lunch money to buy these records.

Our company was the first to introduce recordings to Waynesville. Then the unknown happened, the world of television.

Our company was among the first to introduce television to Waynesville. There were other television companies.

Television hit with a bang. Our closest stations were in Charlotte and Atlanta.

The signal was very spotty. Some sections the signal could not be picked up. There had to be antennas to pick up the signal.

This began the time when we had to hire service men to install antennas.

8-track tapes had become popular. Up until this time the wire recorders were used.

Customers were very confused as to how to get televisions to work in their home. Everyone wanted to know. They couldn't believe they could see and listen to someone in their living room.

Some real interesting stories came from the early television days.

Customers were trying to find better television signals. They would say, "We used an old bicycle wheel and we got it better," One customer said, "We put tinfoil on the lead wire and got it." Then another would say, "We were walking along and fell in a ditch and that's where the antenna is."

All the antennas had to be grounded. One particular lady had a small fenced yard with a cow in it. She said, "Go ahead and put the antenna on the chimney and guy it down in the pasture," which was her yard.

One Sunday afternoon she came to our house and told us that the cow got hung up in the guy wires and pulled the chimney off the house.

One person took a look at the antenna tower in the store and wanted to know if that was the television. Another took a set home and after a few days she came back to the shop and said, "It works. I think I will buy it, but I can't come to town every week to get the films."

One customer said, "My television works good but I want you to take the Arthur Godfrey tube out."

A guy kept having trouble with his television set and said, "If my television tears up again I'm going to throw it off the bank." His television tore up again and he threw it off the bank. He came carrying it in. He had it in two-bushel baskets. It couldn't be repaired.

One lady declared, "I have broken the picture tube and if you don't have one, my husband will be an unhappy man." She had pushed a piece of furniture in it and had broken the safety glass, which was easy to repair.

One guy found out if he beat on the television he could get the sound back on. Out of anger, he had beat a little too hard and had a hole in the side of the cabinet.

On one occasion, a lady calls to say her set was smoking. Her request was to repair it before General Hospital came on. The serviceman arrives at her house while General Hospital is on. She couldn't see it but she could hear it.

The smoke was filling the room. He said, "Lady you had better turn the set off, your will have every part in it burned up." She said, "Wait a minute until I see what Audrey does."

This brings back some memories of repairing the early radios. One lady was bringing her radio to the shop to be repaired. Someone gave her a ride. She said, "The tube next to the Waynesville Station is burned out".

To pick up a radio signal in the early days, a wire was run out the window and sometimes connected to an antenna. You could pick up better signal if you held your hand to the aerial wire. One guy thought if that's so, he'd put a piece of fat meat inside the radio. The fat meat melted on the tubes and ruined the radio.

All the black and white televisions were out. They were all in color now.

The old beer cans, tinfoil and fat meat were out for making the signal better. Every one got antennas, towers and then cable television. We also had closer television stations and relay stations on the mountains.

The tapes have changed from quads to cassettes.

By the time we had closed our shop, the tubes were out and printed circuits were in. The parts were more perfected and television sets were better. There were satellite dishes for better signals. Close of the year 1984.

This was some of the big changes as television entered the world of changes.

Donated Photo

A crank up Graph-a-phone

Shows when the Hi Fidelity players could use all speeds: 78, 45, and 33 1/3 rpm. The adapter in center was for 45 rpm.

An old floor model radio displayed where the family gathered so all could hear the programs.

Waynesville Drive In

In the early years there was a silent movie on Main Street in Waynesville, owned by Mr. Massie.

Then there were the years when movies could be shown with sound. Over the years there were street theaters and drive-in theaters.

Like the television this was a big change.

Waynesville still has one of the drive-in theaters in business. There is one more in existence in North Carolina. It is in the Eastern part of the state

James (Teaberry) Clark, and his wife Ruth Clark has worked in the movie theater business since an early age, James being 15, and Ruth 26 at the time.

In August 1949, The Waynesville outdoor theater opened for business. Waynesville had one more outdoor theater at this time (Smoky Mountain Theater). There were outdoor theaters all around as well as street theaters.

This was where everyone went for entertainment. Television was just beginning.

Each person was given a pair of 3-Dimension glasses to watch some of the movies.

James and Ruth's outdoor theater can accommodate 250 cars and other spaces can be used since the sky monitors brings the sound through the car instead of using the outside speakers.

The film comes in rolls of five. James transfers these to large rolls that will fit the projector. He works an hour getting them on the large roll and getting them adjusted for a good clear outdoors picture.

A carload of people can attend the theater for $8.00.

The theater has a modern up to date concession stand serving the new snacks of now days.

This business has survived for 50 plus years. There have been some changes in outdoor theater business.

Only two of these screens can be found in North Carolina at this time. This is really something of the past. From silent movies, to large, modern movies.

James Clark showing the reels that come in making the movie. Reels must be separated.

Mrs. James Clark (Ruth) in the now days concession stand at the Wayneville Theater.

The Great Depression

By Mazie K. Gerringer

The Great Depression years were most of the 1920s and 1930s and continued until 1941. These were the years my siblings and I were growing up as children.

We lived from the crops that we grew. Therefore, we still had enough food. In fact, we grew and preserved more food from the crops. We raised and killed more hogs. We had an extra milk cow. There was plenty of milk and butter. We had more chickens. Therefore, we had a few extra ones to sell and we sold eggs, also. We still had clothes made of feed and flour sacks. We took extra pain in taking care of our clothes.

We had no money to lose. We still received money from a portion of tobacco sales. We sold some pigs, hog meat, chickens and eggs to buy necessary items such as sugar, salt, coffee and etc.

We children picked beans to earn a small amount of money. We picked and sold blackberries for 5 cents a gallon. This money was used to buy material for making school clothes.

Since we had no money to lose, we survived better than the ones having money.

The Great Depression was felt all over the United States. Banks closed, insurance companies failed and businesses had to lock their doors.

On top of all of that, the great droughts of 1934-1936 burned acres of land and the entire states were turned into dust bowls.

The winds blew for nine days and took away four inches of topsoil in one place. Roads had to be closed. As a result of this cows and horses had to be sold because most of the grazing land was gone.

Millions of grasshoppers devoured the crops. Corn was sold for ten cents a bushel. Whole ears of corn were put into the furnaces instead of wood.

Everyone that lived through the depression can 't forget the terrible toll it took on the nation.

Widespread rumors caused many people to withdraw all their life savings before the banks closed. Others chose to wait and they lost everything they had. The wealthy were hit first but it wasn't long before everyone felt its effects. There were no available jobs. The highways of our nation were filled with men looking for work. Some of them were young men who had just graduated from school and college. These should have been looking forward to a bright future.

The successful men that had good jobs had to start looking for work. Since there was no money, they couldn't travel to look for work. Many men became hobos. These were men who rode boxcars or on top of the train in all kinds of weather. Railroad detectives kept a sharp eye out for them and put them off. Some of them who left for work depended on charities to help them.

The Salvation Army provided milk for the children. There would be long lines for each child bringing their own cup to get milk.

The number of people out of work during these years was ten million or thirty five per cent of all Americans.

The worst influenza outbreak in history claimed the lives of 500,000 people during these years.

When Franklin D. Roosevelt was elected as president he began to put programs into effect that would provide jobs and things began to look better. In 1933 he started the Civilian Conservation Corporation (CCC). This work relief program helped to build roads, restore public lands, build bridges and parks, fight forest fires, and help with disaster relief. The CCC was run like a military camp. It gave work to nearly three million men. These men were paid $30.00 a month, with $25.00 of this being sent back to their family. They had a place to sleep, warm clothes, and food. Some men stayed on this job for six years. Many were able to finish their high school education while they were there. The WPA was started at this time also and many men were lucky enough to get the job helping build roads. Our father worked for WPA and made fifty cents a day.

Families had to have a lot of courage, strength and love to get them through a time like this.

This was a time of changes in the whole United States.

Adjusting To Changes

This is how my Grandparents, Wiley and Dollie had to adjust to life when they moved to town.

After convincing Grandma and Grandpa that they should move to town with us, he wondered about having his chickens and hogs. He tried this for the first year. Then we had a hard time convincing him that it was cheaper to buy meat and eggs than to buy the feed to feed them.

Grandma adjusted well. She visited with us some and we told her what life was like away from the farm.

We had to realize this was all new to them. We had several years to get adjusted to the changes. Our mama had adjusted well also in the years since she moved with us to town.

Since neither of them could read nor write it was hard to explain just what all the new appliances would do for them. After all the only electric items they had before moving were an iron and the electric lights.

Some of the questions asked by Grandpa were: "How is the water getting in and out of the house?" They were used to a spring with water having to be carried in. "How can it be hot and cold?" "Where is the spring?" It was so amazing to them to wash dishes in a sink and let the water out. "Where is the water going?" He was shown the septic tank that held the waste. "Where do you put wood in the heater and the cook stove?" The heater was oil with the oil barrel holding the oil. The stove was electric.

Grandpa did not have to cut wood anymore. That was hard for him to believe. That had been a job all his life.

Grandpa was taken under the house and was shown the pipes that ran the water in and the water out. He was shown the oil line that came from the oil barrel.

We hadn't had a telephone long. We tried to explain to both of them, that in case of an emergency that they could dial "0" and get help. Of course the change now is "911." The first time Grandpa answered the telephone he said, " What do you want?" We had let him listen to voices on the telephone. It was unbelievable to him.

These were the changes with my grandparents. Just like their grandchildren did, our grandchildren have to tell us as grandparents the things of today. For instance: the computer, the telephone, VCR, microwave, clocks, radios and much more.

Everything is controlled by dialing or clicking on the right positions.

Grandpa Wiley Caldwell
Grandma Dollie Caldwell
The years when they adjusted to town life.

Fifty-Six Years Of Changes In Waynesville & Haywood County

As I remember them-Mazie K. Gerringer

May 4, 1944 I graduated from Fines Creek High School. These were the years that high school finished with eleven years. Children could start school at the age of 5. My class had nine girls and one boy. Some of the boys had gone to service the year before. The total school enrollment, grades 1-11, was 451 (218 boys and 233 girls). There was no kindergarten. Kindergarten began in the year 1971 in Haywood County Public schools.

Fines Creek was a caring place where children wanted to learn and the teacher encouraged them. The average teacher's salary was $1883.00 per year. School buses were driven by adults and paid 50 cents an hour. School lunches were 10 cents and many children had to eat free. Instead of paying for your lunches, you were allowed to wash dishes in the lunchroom for 1 hour each day. Also the parents could send things from home to cook in exchange for a lunch. For instance, one half-gallon can of green beans or blackberries was worth 35 cents. Meals were special at the Fines Creek School.

Our family was living with our grandparents since my father's death. I was eight years old when we moved with them. My grandparents were tenant farmers. Unfortunately, they had no education.
They could neither read nor write.

Times were very rough in the early 1940s. The Second World War, which began 1941, brought a lot of hardships.

The REA (Rural Electrification Association) had brought electricity to the rural area where we live in 1939. There was a small watt light bulb in each room. A much better light than the kerosene lamp, I must say.

Those who could afford electrical appliances as: stoves, refrigerators, irons found life was much easier. Electric rates were $1.50 per month.

The war years (1941-1945) brought many changes nationwide. A new era in the life of women had begun. Approximately 6 million women who had never worked outside the home joined the labor force. Some women joined the WACS and replaced men behind the military lines. 2500 men and women from Haywood Country were in the armed forces.

On June 1, 1944 I came to Waynesville to work. My first job was a waitress at the Gordon Hotel. My salary was $10.00 a week plus tips. This was great for me, a sixteen year old, who had never had money. Room and board had to be paid out of this. Fortunately, I boarded with my half sister. White uniforms were required and they had to be bought out of this pay.

Hotel rates were $3.00 per day. Most of the hotels served great meals. The tourist came to Waynesville because of the climate and the accommodations.

My next job was at Wellco Shoe Factory. They were making combat boots for the military as well as a line of bedroom slippers. My salary was $16.00 a week before deductions. That was a 40-hour week at 40 cents an hour. Wellco had three shifts with 300 people employed.

Dayton Rubber Mfg. Company (Dayco Products) began in the 1940s and also employed many people. In 1944, this company paid their 800 employees with over one-half ton of new silver dollars.

A siren was blown in town each morning at 6 AM. This alerted the people that it was wake up time to go to work. Sometime in the late 1940s, after the war, this practice was discontinued.

For a number of years in the 1940s, there were city buses that covered the town and for some of the rural area to carry the people to their jobs. The fare was 10 cents in the city limits. Longer rides were 25 to 35 cents. Taxis' covered the area also with a fare of 50 cents in the city limits. Clarence Muse owned one of the first taxicab services. This was helpful to the people. The new cars started coming more around 1945.

Walking was done by lots of folks to save the fares.

Waynesville now had good cafes, some of these with curb service. Curb service was the popular way of getting the new foods. They were: hamburgers, cheeseburgers, hot dogs, french fries, milkshakes, and etc. Charlie's place was the favorite hang out, especially for the teens that wanted to show off their new car.

Waynesville had two dairies Pet and Biltmore that would deliver milk to the home, in glass jars for 70 cents a gallon. Biltmore had the special ice cream bar. This was all new to everyone.

Ray's Super Market was first a food store then it became a super grocery store. The store also became a clothing store. It was a one stop for every thing in foods and clothing.

Waynesville had many businesses like; clothing, shoe stores, drug stores, cafes, shoe repairs, and 5 & 10 cents stores, where merchandise could be bought beginning at 5 and 10 cents.

Many foods were rationed during World War 2. Each family was issued ration stamps. Sugar was one of the things rationed. Sugar Stamps were sometimes sold on the black market to moon shiners. Moon shiners used the sugar in making the white lightning.

Gasoline was also rationed. It was 15 cents a gallon. New tires sold for $7.95 each. The average price for the new cars in 1945-1946 was $1125.00. The Buick's price in 1952 was $2315.88. Some of the cars sold at this time were Mercury, Nash, Packard and Desoto.

Oleomargarine came into existence in the 1940s. The first margarine came with a package of yellow dye that would be mixed with the white margarine. Margarine now days, even though it is a certain percentage of vegetable oil, tastes almost like butter.

Cigarettes were very scarce. All brands sold for 15 cents a pack. The customer was allowed to buy one package at a time.

1940s and 1950s burning trash was allowed at home. Most everyone burned all the newspapers, tree limbs and leaves. A private trash collector would pick up metal, old furniture and etc. for $2.00 a month.

The cost to go to the Movie Theater was 30 cents. Popcorn and fountain cokes at the theater were 10 cents each. The outdoor theaters began. This was the place to go. The Waynesville Drive-In Theater opened 1949 and is still operating this year 2000. Some of the Massie's owned the theaters.

Floyd and Louise Nelson started selling Television around the year 1950. The sets were all black and white. The signal was poor. The stations were too far away for the mountains. They also had the first record shop in Waynesville. The first record players had a record that had a talking speed. The crank up player that my father owned had a cylinder record. The needle was a permanent diamond. Record players, speeds of the records, styles and etc. have changed. The signal and better televisions have changed

In 1963 cable TV came to Waynesville. The antenna was no longer needed.

Telephone service has changed greatly. In 1940s everyone had a party line. Since you could never get on the line, it wasn't much benefit to the folks. The operator had to dial for service needed.

The monthly bill was about $3.00. In 1953 the dial telephone came to Waynesville and replaced the operators.

Answering machines were not heard of.

It was a joyful occasion on August 16, 1945 when approximately 7,000 people came to Waynesville to celebrate the news that the war was over.

These are some of the prices according to national figures in 1946; Average income per year $2500, new house from $5000, to $6000, new car $1125, and a loaf of bread 10 cents. Nylon stockings came on the market in the 1940s. There was only one color and they were rationed. They were advertised as 51 gauge, 15denier, for $1.50 per pair.

Some headlines in 1947: Women in Haywood County were being placed on the jury list for the first time, Waynesville gets 125 parking meters, WHCC was listed as Haywood County's first radio station.

In 1949 a subscription to the Waynesville Mountaineer, a newspaper company, was $3.00 per year. Christmas cards could be mailed for 2 cents if mailed in an unsealed envelope. Post Cards cost 1 cent, regular first class postage was 3 cents, and airmail was 6 cents.

Some of the headlines of 1950 were: Waynesville has a population of 5,288, Fines Creek gets telephones, John Queen builds a 20 unit motor court on Walnut Street, Turner and Son opens a clothing store on Main Street and Haywood citizens owns over 7 million dollars in U.S. Savings Bonds, Building is up in the county with $574, 700 in building permits.

In 1960 a mild building boom continued. Eagle's Nest Mountain, which used to be Junaluska Mountain was developed. The New Year showed 23, 641 registered voters in the County and the tax rate was reduced to $1.88.

A new wing of the Haywood County Hospital was opened with 54 beds. The hospital was located at 1600 N. Main Street. The Haywood County Board Of Education and Social Services occupy this building in the year 2000. The new hospital is now located on Jones Cove Road and is named Haywood Regional Medical Center. It opened in October 1979 with 200 beds.

Waynesville Junior High School had its last graduating class in 1965. This school is now called the Waynesville Middle School. Some of the school was destroyed by fire October 1993. Tuscola High School opened in 1966. In the winter of 1960 the schools closed for sixteen times due to snow. Seven days of that time was made up on Saturdays.

In 1960 Wall Street in Waynesville was widened and paved. The town erected 400 new signposts 16,000 license tags were bought that year.

A 12,000 square foot packing plant was built on Asheville Road near the Haywood County Health Department.

In 1967 the Mt. Sterling School, the last one-room school of Haywood County closed.

A new section of Waynesville was opened in the 1960s called "Russ Avenue", named after Mr. W. Curtis Russ, owner of The Waynesville Mountaineer Paper Company. Waynesville's first shopping center, The Waynesville Plaza, is located there. Some of the new businesses and some of the older businesses moved to this shopping center. They are: Sky City, United 5 & 10 cent Store, Sears Catalog Store, Ingles, Sherwin-Williams, Eckerd's, The Army Store, Family Dollar Store, Winn-Dixie, Radio Shack, and others. Many fast foods opened on Russ Avenue; Kentucky Fried Chicken, Pizza Hut, Burger King, Wendy's and Quincy's.

Another shopping center opened off of Russ Avenue at Barber Blvd. There are new businesses here also.

Russ Avenue has a new motel, Econo Lodge. Oak Park Motel is still operating. On the hill off of Russ Avenue there is a new motel Day's Inn.

Maggie Valley and Lake Junaluska has lots of motels. There are many restaurants and fast food places for dining.

Waynesville and surrounding areas are still very much prepared for the many tourists visiting this area.

Lake Junaluska is surrounded by the beautiful mountains and has a beautiful lake to attract the many Methodist that meet here for conferences. They accommodate the tourists also. This area has changed for the conveniences.

Waynesville and areas around have many golf courses for the golfers.

Haywood County has changed with all the lovely homes.

Waynesville has two modern funeral homes, Garrett's and Wells'. There is also a Wells' in Canton, N.C. Mr. Noble Garrett bought the Massie Funeral Home, which became Garrett's. The Wells family bought the Crawford Funeral Home, which belonged to Theda and Howell Crawford.

Waynesville and Canton have several nursing and retirement homes. A low rent complex called the Towers is located on Church Street where once was Rays' Super Store. There are several low rent apartment units. There are also several Condominiums.

The Salvation Army began here many years ago in a small way and has progressed to a modern building on Pigeon Street. The Haywood Christian Ministry outgrew its facilities and moved to a larger building on Asheville Rd. At this date, year 2000, this building has been bought to make a new highway and they have plans to relocate.

In the early 1970s the Broyhill Orphanage for children was opened. It is located on Jones Cove Rd. It is owned and operated by NC Baptist. The orphanage has 5 cottages with 12 children each and house parents.

A great plus for the schools was when Haywood Technical College opened in the late 1960s. There are specials subjects that the students can take to meet the world of changes. Many subjects are taught here.

In the 1970s there were many changes taking place all over the country:

Computers, satellite dishes, microwaves, air conditioners, curling irons, VCR's, fast foods, and many more.

In the 1980s many changes came about in the field of medicine. Numerous doctors who specialize, new equipment for every need at the hospitals, rescue squads and helicopter service to transport patients on the scene.

Modern techniques came about in dentistry such as dental implants. There were many different fields that opened up in the ways of treating the eyes. Cataract Surgery was one of them. There are many modern means of treating any health problem.

The 1980s showed a big increase in population in the county. There was more construction of homes and businesses.

Computers were introduced and taught in the school classrooms and kindergarten classes.

It was a sad day in June of 1994 when the Fines Creek School closed its doors for the last time. Because of declining enrollment the Haywood County Board of Education made a decision to transport the remaining sixty students to Crabtree-Ironduff School to further their education.

In 120 Years Of Changes we have gone from:
- oil lamps to electric lights
- outside toilet to inside toilet
- carrying water from the spring to running water in the homes
- fireplaces to oil stoves,
- furnace to electric heat;
- oxen to first car to high powered fuel injection engines
- one-room school to modern schools and colleges and to home-schooling
- home remedies of medicine to antibiotics and special medicines;
- country stores to store on wheels to modern super stores
- feather beds and straw ticks to innerspring mattresses to waterbeds
- homemade lye soap to liquid soaps and concentrated detergents
- home killing hogs to slaughter houses to meat

212

factories
- handkerchiefs to Kleenex
- scrub board washing to programmed washing machines
- push lawn mowers to riding mowers
- homemade coffins and home burial to caskets and funeral homes
- corn and flour mills to modern factory grinding and packaging paper bags (pokes) to toe sacks to plastic bags
- heavy black irons to electric irons
- battery radios to electric AM &FM and back to modern convenient battery radios
- wind up graph-a-phone to record players to stereos to compact disc
- three cent postage of letters, one cent post card to airmail to e-mail
- telegraphs to fax machines
- first airplane by the Wright Bothers to jet planes to man on the moon and to many others.

This year 2000, Waynesville has decided with all the cars on the highway that once again they need another wider highway into town. (Business 23, Asheville Rd).

Changes are too numerous to mention since electricity came. We have only mentioned a few.

196. Haywood County Courthouse, Waynesville,
     1932

195. Armory, Waynesville, 1936

21. Ratcliffe farm house, Ratcliffe Cove, 1865-1878

22. Joshua Kinsland house, Bethel, 1863

Courtesy-Haywood Homes and History. In the middle of the 1800's until the turn of the century, large frame homes were popular.

64. Walnut Street house, No. 306, Waynesville,
c.1930

65. Kirkpatrick Apartments, Walnut Street,
Waynesville, c.1930

Courtesy-Haywood Homes and History. As the town grew,
so did the building of new homes and apartments.

216

Think Back With Us
120 years ago

Think back with us to this time. Life was simple because there were not so many things to remember as to how to work all the machines that helps to make our life easier.

This was before jet planes, man on the moon, TV, VCR's, computers, cellular phones, fax machines, wonder drugs, modern machines, yogurt, pizza, macaroni, spaghetti, instant coffee, silk stockings, fast foods, xerox, split atoms, laser beams, contact lenses, plastic, ballpoint pins, clothes dryers, washing machines, electric blankets, air conditioners, drip-dry clothes, before man walked on the moon, the pill, and much, much, more.

Folks got married first and then lived together. In these years, rabbits were not Volkswagons.

No wonder we need someone to help us get all this and more straightened out in our minds.

Every thing is controlled by push buttons and click on machines. The time we save is used in learning how to do all these new machines.

Changes are necessary and sometimes from one generation to another bringing with it new ideas and inventions. The world we live in is in constant changes, almost hourly.

Some say we have already reached the age of completion and perfection. We have not. Things change for the better. So, we will change with it. But, we must take time to get caught up first.

What will be beyond the year 2000?

Remembering Way Back When

Mazie K. Gerringer

Do you remember when people visited each other? A visit was a quiet, simple time that we spent with others. This time was usually unannounced, and you didn't expect to be entertained. You talked, laughed, joked, and cried together. This was a time to learn all the needs of your fellowman.

Visiting is announced now days. Everyone is in a hurry.

Do you remember when you really felt safe in your home, car or on the street? Years ago when I grew up in the country, our house didn't have locks on the windows nor doors. Those who had locks did not have the need to use them.

My, how things have changed! Deadbolt locks, security lights, and burglar alarms don't give us peace of mind anymore.

Do you remember when children went barefoot? On the first day of May, our parents gave us permission to go barefoot. It didn't matter if it was very cold, such as blackberry winter. This was the time we started going barefoot every year. By this time our shoes were worn out.

Do you remember when many items of clothing as we know them today were called something entirely different? Pants were called britches. Ladies dress shoes or slippers were called pumps. Socks were called anklets. Ladies underwear was called bloomers. A bra was called a brassiere. A girdle was called a corset. A blouse was called a waist.

Do you remember when most housewives wore aprons? Aprons were part of the everyday attire. My Grandma and Mother wore an apron until their death.

Do you remember when women didn't wear slacks (pants)? Women's style of dress changed a lot during war years, 1941-1945. This was the time that many women went to work in factories and they were allowed to wear slacks. In fact, slacks were encouraged to wear in the factories to help prevent getting dresses caught in machinery. A few years later pantsuits became fashionable. This was different.

Today it's hard to tell women's clothes from men's in some cases.

Do you remember when most women wore bonnets and hats? You seldom ever saw a woman in church without a hat. In 1960 this changed. Hairstyles begin to change drastically by then. Women left the hats off to show off the new hairstyle. Long, braided hair, which was so prominent then, is almost a thing of the past.

If you can remember all these things you are a senior citizen. You are hopefully enjoying a more relaxed lifestyle.

If you don't remember all these things you need to talk with your grandparents. They will tell you all the wonderful things you have missed.

Note from the Co-author-
Mazie Kinsland Gerringer

After my sister, Louise Kinsland Nelson, wrote the books, "Country Folklore", "The Aroma and Memories Of Grandma's & Mama's Kitchen", "Horse Drawn Equipment & Early Tools", and "Historic Waynesville and Haywood County", I realized how important it was for future generations to know these things. These books made me aware of all the changes that had taken place in my lifetime. As a result we decided to write "120 Years Of Changes".

What a difference a day makes, a week, a month, a year or fifty years! It's almost unbelievable the changes that took place in the last 120 Years.

In the late 1800s and early 1900s life was very simple as compared to today. Many things changed with the invention of the automobile. Electricity probably brought more changes than any other thing. We couldn't keep up with all the changes it brought about. Then came computers that changed the whole world. The internet, cyber space, e-mail and cellular phones are great. Fifty-six years ago no one in their wildest imagination would have thought of all these accomplishments.

What changes will take place in the next 120 years for someone to write about? Maybe faster jet planes, pleasure trips to the moon, a cure-all for every disease known to man, no poverty in the world, no crime, and peace on earth.

Note from Co-author Louise Kinsland Nelson

I've been asked what inspired me to write about the days gone by.

The answer is, "I Love It". It's a history that needs to be handed down to generations after us.

When I was writing for The Enterprise Mountaineer, the parents and grandparents were trying to save the clippings. They encouraged me to get the writings in a book so they could hand it down to their children and grandchildren.

I have four books prior to this book, "120 Years Of Changes". My sister, Mazie Kinsland Gerringer is co-authoring this book with me.

My books," Country Folklore", "The Aroma & Memories Of Grandma's & Mama's Kitchen", "Horse Drawn Equipment & Early Tools", and "Historic Waynesville & Haywood County", have been a success.

"120 Years of Changes", tells how life was a struggle for my Grandpa's parents in 1880 and then a struggle for his life through the next years. Since there was no school in the area where they grew up, they had no education. This made living very hard for both he and Grandma. Plus living in the years without electricity made it extra hard. This goes into the years when he moved to town to begin a life with electricity.

They went through all these years with changes. The way of living in the country and town had many changes.

My siblings and I grew up in the years of 1920s-1930s. Life was hard for us. We learned to share, to love, to respect, to manage and to cope with life. We survived.

Each of you has special memories and a different style of living from your grandchildren. I would like to encourage you to write, tape or have some one to write these memories for your children and grandchildren. We are the last generation that lived these years. After us it will be hearsay. Help preserve history.

References and Years

References with pictures
Haywood county Homes and History by Betsy Farlow, Dan Lane
and Duane Oliver
Haywood County Courthouse 1932-ref #196-page 214
Waynesville Armory 1936-ref #195-page 214
Moody Farm Log Barn, Upper Fines Creek, 19th Century-ref #5,
page 148
Jim Hannah Log House, Little Cataloochee 1864-ref #3
Shook Smathers House, Clyde, NC 1795-ref #1, page 152
Patton House, Canton, NC 1830s-ref #2, page 152
Waldo Green House, Fines Creek 1930-ref #163, page 150
Kirkpatrick Apartments, Walnut Street, Waynesville, NC 1930-ref
#21, page 216
Ratcliffe Farm House, Ratcliffe Cove, Waynesville, NC 1865-
1878-ref # 21, page 215
Joshua Kinsland House, Bethel 1863-ref #22, page 215
McCracken-Palmer House, Fines Creek, 1860-ref #11, page 116
Richland Rolling Mill, Lake Jusaluska, NC -ref #198, page 65
Walnut Street House, Waynesville, NC 1930-ref #22, 164, page
216
Heritage of Healing: A Medical History of Haywood County by
Nina L. Anderson and William L. Anderson
Dr. H. H. Way's Office, Waynesville, NC page 134
Dr. J. F. Abel's Office, Waynesville, NC page 134
Dr. Robert Lee Walker, Crabtree, page 135
Waynesville's First Hospital, Pigeon Street, page 133
Champion Hospital, Canton, NC page 136
James Clark & Ruth Clark-story of The Waynesville Drive-In, page
193
Theda Crawford-1940 Basketball Team, page 177
Baptizing in the creek, page 160

Doyle Brown-cross cut saw-page 43
Deddie Parker-apple pie and dried apples, page 109
Waynesville Mountaineer
    Old timers with horse buggy, page 139
    Old Kenmore Hotel, page 135
    White Sulphur Springs Hotel, page 135
    Street Changes, page 180
    Eagles Nest Hotel
Ann Kinsland-Old barn by the side of the road, page 149
    Old barn with a tin roof, page 155, 157
Bill Buchanan-Sheep, page76
    Barbwire fence & split wood, page 104
King Family-Old log house, page 5
John Francis-Old car, page
    Buggy, page 42
Charlie Massie & Pauline Massie-Very old crank churn, page 89
    Cabbage cutter & Sausage mill, page 67
    Jerry Massie's log house, page 119
    Jerry Massie's Old buildings, 120, 121, 122, 123
Bob Allen-Old shed, page 153
    Rock apple house, page 154
    Barn & silo, page 156
    Modern day barn, page 158
Kelly Farm, Crabtree-chickens, page 99
    Farm equipment, page 87
    Molasses making, page 103
Katherine Wells Jackson-Wash pot, page 79
    Cooking pots, page 57
Benton McCrary-picture of Wiley Caldwell & Bill McCrary,
page 116
Joyce Rogers-Crabtree Post Office, page 126
    Earlier Crabtree Post Office, page 128
Many other pictures and memories by a variety of people

Information:

Haywood Homes & History by Betsy Farlow, Dan Lane and Duane Oliver
Heritage of Healing: A Medical History of Haywood county by Nina L. Anderson & William L. Anderson
James Clark & Ruth Clark-History of the Waynesville Drive In Theater
W. Clark Medford's Early History of Haywood County
Joyce Rogers, information and pictures of the early Crabtree, NC Postal Service

Ordering Information

Country Folklore
1920 & 1930
...and that's the way it was.
Louise K. Nelson
1336 Asheville Rd.
Waynesville, N.C. 28786
828-456-3760 or 828-456-8076

(A). Country Folklore-1920s-1930s   Customs of Country Living. Living without electricity, going to the one-room school, Use of animals around the farm, 1936 snow, Country Stores and more.

(B). The Aroma Of Grandma's & Mama's Kitchen
Cooking and history of Grandma's cooking when she used a dib of this and a pinch of that. Going through the years of canning. Recipes as: apple stack cake, crackling bread, and simple cooking then to the canning recipes of chow-chow,

226

(C). Horse Drawn Equipment & Early Tools, pictures and description, cost per book $10.95 NC Tax $0.66 shipping $3.00

To   order   list   how   many
(A)$12.95_____(B)$12.95_____(C)$10.95_____
Cost per book $12.95- NC Tax $0.78 -shipping $3.00 per book
When ordering 2 books shipping $4.00- 3 books, shipping $5.00
Total   books   cost____   NC
Tax____shipping_____Total_____

(D) Historic Waynesville is a hardback book, 226 pages with many pictures, cost per book $29.95 NC Tax $1.80, shipping $5.00
List   how   many_____,   NC
Tax_____shipping_____Total_____

(E).120 Years Of Changes, cost per book $12.95_____NC Tax $0.78___shipping_$3.00____
 List how many_____N.C.Tax_____shipping_____
                                                  _____
          Complete   cost: Total   NC
          Tax_____shipping_____
Deduct N.C. Tax when out of state___
Name   Phone_____
          Date_____
Address_____Zip_____

Index